**New Directions for
Child and Adolescent
Development**

Lene Arnett Jensen
Reed W. Larson
EDITORS-IN-CHIEF

William Damon
FOUNDING EDITOR

D1525571

Focus on Gender:
Parent and Child
Contributions to
the Socialization of
Emotional Competence

Amy Kennedy Root
Susanne A. Denham
EDITORS

Number 128 • Summer 2010
Jossey-Bass
San Francisco

Focus on Gender: Parent and Child Contributions to the Socialization of Emotional Competence
Amy Kennedy Root, Susanne A. Denham (eds.)
New Directions for Child and Adolescent Development, no. 128
Lene Arnett Jensen, Reed W. Larson, Editors-in-Chief

Microfilm copies of issues and articles are available in 16mm and 35mm, as well as microfiche in 105mm, through University Microfilms, Inc., 300 North Zeeb Road, Ann Arbor, Michigan 48106-1346.

ISSN 1520-3247   electronic ISSN 1534-8687

NEW DIRECTIONS FOR CHILD AND ADOLESCENT DEVELOPMENT is part of The Jossey-Bass Education Series and is published quarterly by Wiley Subscription Services, Inc., a Wiley company, at Jossey-Bass, 989 Market Street, San Francisco, California 94103-1741. Periodicals postage paid at San Francisco, California, and at additional mailing offices. Postmaster: Send address changes to New Directions for Child and Adolescent Development, Jossey-Bass, 989 Market Street, San Francisco, CA 94103-1741.

New Directions for Child and Adolescent Development is indexed in Cambridge Scientific Abstracts (CSA/CIG), CHID: Combined Health Information Database (NIH), Contents Pages in Education (T&F), Current Abstracts (EBSCO), Educational Research Abstracts Online (T&F), ERIC Database (Education Resources Information Center), Index Medicus/MEDLINE/PubMed (NLM), Linguistics & Language Behavior Abstracts (CSA/CIG), Psychological Abstracts/PsycINFO (APA), Social Services Abstracts (CSA/CIG), SocINDEX (EBSCO), and Sociological Abstracts (CSA/CIG).

SUBSCRIPTION rates: For the U.S., $85 for individuals and $299 for institutions. Please see ordering information page at end of journal.

EDITORIAL CORRESPONDENCE should be e-mailed to the editors-in-chief: Lene Arnett Jensen (ljensen@clarku.edu) and Reed W. Larson (larsonr@ illinois.edu).

Contents

Kennedy Root, A., & Denham, S. A. (2010). The role of gender in the socialization of emotion: Key concepts and critical issues. In A. Kennedy Root & S. Denham (Eds.), *The role of gender in the socialization of emotion: Key concepts and critical issues. New Directions for Child and Adolescent Development*, 128, 1–9. San Francisco: Jossey-Bass.

1

The Role of Gender in the Socialization of Emotion: Key Concepts and Critical Issues

Amy Kennedy Root, Susanne A. Denham

Abstract

Given the omnipresent role of gender in children's and adolescents' development, it seems necessary to better understand how gender affects the process of emotion socialization. In this introductory chapter, the authors discuss the overarching themes and key concepts discussed in this volume, as well as outline the distinct contribution of each individual chapter. Each chapter within this volume underscores the important role that parents play in the socialization of emotion, and the impact gender-typed emotion socialization may have on later socioemotional adjustment. © Wiley Periodicals, Inc.

Emotions play a pivotal role in a multitude of areas of child and adolescent development, including social functioning, academic performance, and the development of psychopathology. Given the primary role that emotion plays across a wide range of developmental processes, it should not be surprising that researchers have focused on understanding the development of emotion over the past twenty years (see Izard, Youngstrom, Fine, Mostow, & Trentacosta, 2006 for relevant review). Although emotions are—in part—biological, the meanings of emotions and appropriateness of emotional expression are socialized; and, in the early years of life, socialization primarily takes place via interactions within the family, and characteristics of both parents and children may affect the process of emotion socialization. Gender is one critically important moderator of what and how children learn about emotion because culture determines the appropriateness of emotional displays for males and females.

Although it is known that mothers and fathers differ in their responses to children's emotions and that they differentiate their responses to emotions by child gender, we are only beginning to understand how these processes may be influenced by other factors and how they may predict later socioemotional development. Thus, a volume devoted to the topic of gender and the socialization of emotional competence seems timely.

The Development of Emotional Competence

When considering affective development, it is important to acknowledge that emotion encompasses a plethora of processes. Many researchers have focused on three areas of emotional development—the *understanding of emotion*, the *expression of emotion*, and the *regulation of emotion* (Denham, Bassett, & Wyatt, 2007; Eisenberg, Cumberland, & Spinrad, 1998; Saarni, 1985). *Emotion understanding* is thought to include both the comprehension of emotional experience, as well as the understanding of others' emotional expressions (Denham et al., 2003; Eisenberg and others, 1998). The *expression of emotion* has been defined as the propensity to display emotions in an effective and appropriate manner within given contexts and cultures (Denham et al., 2003; Eisenberg et al., 1998). Finally, the *regulation of emotion* has been defined as "the extrinsic and intrinsic processes responsible for monitoring, evaluating, and modifying emotional reactions to accomplish one's goals" (Thompson, 1994, p. 27).

Together, emotion understanding, emotion expression, and emotion regulation are thought to encompass the larger construct of *emotional competence* (Denham et al., 2003, 2007; Eisenberg et al., 1998). *Emotional competence* has been associated with processes beyond affective development, including the expression of socially competent behavior (Denham et al., 2003; Schmidt, DeMulder, & Denham, 2002) and

NEW DIRECTIONS FOR CHILD and ADOLESCENT DEVELOPMENT • DOI: 10.1002/cd

academic performance (Trentacosta & Izard, 2007). Although emotion understanding, expression, and regulation are collectively necessary for adaptive development, researchers have also demonstrated that each of these processes contributes separately to successful socioemotional development. For example, the ability to effectively understand emotions is paramount in the development of empathetic and sympathetic responding (Eisenberg, 2000; Zahn-Waxler, 2000). The expression of emotion is an essential part of social signaling and communication; this set of skills is particularly important in the early years of life when language skills have not fully developed (Tronick, Cohn, & Shea, 1986). Finally, the development of emotion regulation skills has been linked to a wide range of indices of adjustment and maladjustment including social competence and likeability in the peer group (for example, Denham et al., 2003), externalizing difficulties (for example, Cole et al., 1996), internalizing difficulties (for example, Rubin, Coplan, Fox, & Calkins, 1995), and the development of psychopathology (for example, Cicchetti, Ackerman, & Izard, 1995).

According to Denham et al. (2007), children learn about emotions via three primary modes of socialization: (a) witnessing others' feelings and emotions, (b) having their emotional displays responded to, and (c) the ways they are taught about their feelings and emotions. These forms of socialization are thought to impact children in direct and indirect ways (Denham, Mitchell-Copeland, Strandberg, Auerbach, & Blair, 1997; Eisenberg et al., 1998). Indirect socialization is thought to occur from the emotional climate within the family unit (Halberstadt, Crisp, & Eaton, 1999) and via parents' own expressiveness of emotion during family interaction (Valiente, Fabes, Eisenberg, & Spinrad, 2004). The expression of emotion within the family unit affords children with the opportunity to witness others' emotional expressions and evaluate the responses others receive after the display of specific emotions. Thus, when children watch the other family members display fear or anger, they gather information about the level of appropriateness for specific emotions. Indeed, children appear to internalize the information they gather from their family's affective climate. There is support for the relation between family expressiveness of emotion and child and adolescent emotional expressiveness and understanding (see Halberstadt and others, 1999 for review), as well as literature to suggest that family expressiveness of emotion impacts the development of emotion regulation (see Morris, Silk, Steinberg, Myers, & Robinson, 2007).

Direct socialization is thought to occur via parental reactions to emotions or parental discussion of emotions with their children. Typically, researchers have examined the different ways that parents respond to their children's emotions, and how different types of reactions affect children's social and emotional development. Parents' responses to children's emotions are typically characterized as supportive or nonsupportive. Supportive reactions include warm, sensitive responses to children's emotions and have been associated with less negative emotionality (Crockenberg, 1987) and emotion understanding (Denham et al., 1997). Nonsupportive reactions, on the other hand, are described as punitive or dismissive responses to children's emotions (Eisenberg et al., 1998) and have been associated with emotion dysregulation, low levels of emotional expression, and less emotion understanding (Denham et al., 1997; Eisenberg & Fabes, 1994).

Of course, the socialization of emotion is impacted by other factors, including characteristics of both parents and children. One such characteristic is gender. The influence of gender is thought to be all-encompassing, and it has been stated that, "Virtually all of human functioning has a gendered cast—appearance, mannerisms, communication, temperament, activities at home and outside, aspirations, and values" (Ruble, Martin, & Berenbaum, 2006, p. 858). Thus, gender would seem to be an important factor to consider when examining the development of emotion.

Gender development is thought to be influenced by a multitude of factors (Ruble et al., 2006), including biology, cognition, and culture. One important way that children learn the rules for being a boy or a girl is via socialization by caretakers (Leaper, 2002). Indeed, parents' attitudes about gender roles (Tenenbaum & Leaper, 2002) and encouragement of gender-typed behaviors (Lytton & Romney, 1991) influence children's beliefs about gender and subsequent gender-typed behavior. Further, mothers and fathers also differ from one another in the ways they communicate with their children (see Leaper, Anderson, & Sanders, 1998 for review) and differ in the ways that they speak to and with their sons and their daughters (Fivush, 1989).

Parents socialize boys' and girls' emotions differently as the norms within a particular culture dictate the masculinity or femininity of specific emotions (Brody, 2000; Underwood, Coie, & Herbsman, 1992). In Western cultures, there is evidence that the expression of sadness and other internalizing affects are perceived to be nonmasculine in college-aged individuals. Men who display such emotions are viewed more negatively than women who display the same affect (Siegel & Alloy, 1990). On the other hand, emotions of an externalizing nature, such as anger, are considered more acceptable in males than females (Birnbaum & Croll, 1984). For instance, aggressive boys are viewed as more likeable by their peers than nonaggressive boys (Serbin et al., 1993), whereas aggressive girls are typically viewed more negatively than nonaggressive girls (Crick, 1997).

Therefore it should not be surprising that researchers have shown that parents encourage different emotions in their sons and daughters. For instance, mothers emphasize sadness and fear in conversations with their daughters, but not their sons (Adams, Kuebli, Boyle, & Fivush, 1995;

Fivush, 1989; Fivush, Brotman, Buckner, & Goodman, 2000). Further, when asked to discuss past events with their children, mothers discussed being angry with their young sons, but not their young daughters (Fivush, 1989). Moreover, there is also evidence that mothers and fathers differ from one another in their responses to children's emotions. For instance, Cassano. Perry-Parrish, and Zeman (2007) reported that fathers responded to their children's sadness with minimizing responses ("Don't be such a cry baby.") more than mothers. In the same study, mothers reported that they would encourage ("It's okay to be upset.") their children's sadness more than fathers would. Thus, it seems reasonable to conclude that (a) parents encourage and discourage different emotions in their sons versus their daughters, and (b) mothers and fathers differ in the types of socialization strategies they utilize with their children. Although there is empirical work to suggest that these differences exist, we are just beginning to understand both the intricacies of these differences and how these differences impact the development of children's emotional competence.

In this volume, new directions and fresh perspectives on the role of gender in the development of emotional competence will be discussed. Each chapter will focus on a distinct area of gender and emotion socialization, all while contributing to the broad focus of this volume: *understanding how and why gender plays a role in the development of children's and adolescents' emotional competence*. In Chapter Two, Chaplin and colleagues examine gender and emotion socialization in an understudied population: low-income families. In Chapter Three, Denham and colleagues discuss the role of mothers and fathers in direct and indirect socialization of emotional expression, understanding, and regulation. Few studies have examined the socialization of specific negative (for example, fear and anger) and positive (for example, happiness) emotions by both mothers and fathers; Kennedy Root and Rubin examine these processes in Chapter Four. The literature on parental emotion socialization is largely focused on the early childhood years, and has left many to question how (and if) parents impact gender and emotional development beyond the early childhood years. Chapters Five and Six focus on this understudied age range. Zeman and colleagues address the role of gender in parent–child discussion of anger and sadness in middle childhood. Brand and Klimes-Dougan consider emotion socialization in adolescence, with a focus on the implications that gender-typed emotion socialization may have on individuals as they transition to adulthood. Finally, in Chapter Seven, Zahn-Waxler provides a closing commentary and outlines future directions for this area of study.

Several major themes are carried throughout the volume. They represent what we feel are some of the critical issues to better understanding the role of gender in emotion socialization and the development of emotional competence.

The Role of Fathers. The majority of the empirical work on gender differences in emotion socialization has involved maternal emotion socialization, with far fewer studies including the role of fathers. In the studies that have been conducted with fathers, it seems that fathers may play a distinct role in children's emotional development (for example, Cassano et al., 2007; Feldman, 2003); however, we are only beginning to understand how fathers socialize emotions, and how paternal emotion socialization impacts children's socioemotional development. Thus, it seems critical to better understand the role of fathers in emotion socialization and the development of emotional competence. Each of the chapters in this volume includes a commentary on the role of fathers in emotion socialization, and many (Chapters Three to Six) provide new empirical evidence for the unique—and important—role fathers play in children's emotional development.

The Socialization of Discrete Emotions. Over the past fifteen years, studies of emotion socialization have allowed for a better understanding of the development of affective behavior. However, much of the existing work is limited because there has been little focus on the socialization of specific emotions (for example, studying responses to anxiety and anger rather than an aggregate of negative emotions). Given that parents respond differently to how boys and girls display of the same emotion, it seems important to examine specific emotions when considering the role of gender in emotion socialization.

The Examination of Emotion Socialization Across Developmental Periods. As mentioned, a large portion of the empirical literature on the topic of emotion socialization has been focused on the infant through early childhood years. However, there is a growing interest in socialization of emotion in the middle childhood and early adolescent years (for example, the 2007 special issue of *Social Development: Emotion Socialization in Childhood and Adolescence*). With this interest in understanding the emotion socialization in older children and adolescents, it seems crucial to better understand the similarities and differences in parental emotion socialization from the early years of life through adolescence.

The Impact of Gender-Differentiated Socialization. Although there is a growing body of research on the role of gender in emotion socialization, the consequences of reinforcing different emotional expressions in boys and girls are still relatively understudied. Several researchers have argued that the different rules (and the resulting differing reactions) for boys' versus girls' emotional expression may result in maladaptive development for some children, especially those at risk. For instance, if a parent reprimands his or her son for expressing fear, the child may eventually learn to inhibit his display of fear; however, he may still *feel* fearful, but simply not *display* it (Buck, 1984). Consequently, the inhibition of his fear may lead to internal dysregulation, which may set the stage for the development of maladjustment—socially, emotionally, and academically.

NEW DIRECTIONS FOR CHILD and ADOLESCENT DEVELOPMENT • DOI: 10.1002/cd

Further, empirical evidence has illuminated the different ways that mothers and fathers react to different emotions in their sons and daughters; however, we are only beginning to understand the potentially unique roles that fathers and mothers play in their children's emotional development.

Conclusion

The goal of this sourcebook is to provide a comprehensive volume raising—and addressing—what we see as the critical issues in the study of gender, emotion socialization, and the development of emotional competence. Each of the chapters provides evidence for the pervasive role that gender plays in emotional development and provides a framework of how to better understand the development of emotion in boys and girls.

References

Adams, S., Kuebli, J., Boyle, P. A., & Fivush, R. (1995). Gender differences in parent-child conversations about past emotions: A longitudinal investigation. *Sex Roles, 33*, 309–323.

Birnbaum, D. W., Nosanchuk, T. A., & Croll, W. L. (1980). Children's stereotypes about sex differences in emotionality. *Sex Roles, 6*, 435–443.

Brody, L. R. (2000). The socialization of gender differences in emotional expression: Display rules, infant temperament, and differentiation. In A. H. Fischer (Ed.), *Gender and emotion: Social psychological perspectives* (pp. 24–47). Cambridge, UK: Cambridge University Press.

Buck, R. (1984). *The Communication of emotion.* New York: Guildford.

Cassano, M., Perry-Parrish, C., & Zeman, J. (2007). Influence of gender on parental socialization of children's sadness regulation. *Social Development, 16*, 210–231.

Cicchetti, D., Ackerman, B. P., and Izard, C. E. (1995). Emotions and emotion regulation in developmental psychopathology. *Development and Psychopathology, 7*, 1–10.

Cole, P. M., Zahn-Waxler, C., Fox, N. A., Usher, B. A., & Welsh, J. D. (1996). Individual differences in emotion regulation and behavior problems in preschool children. *Journal of Abnormal Psychology, 105*, 518–529.

Crick, N. (1997). Engagements in gender normative versus nonnormative forms of aggression: Links to social-psychological adjustment. *Developmental Psychology, 33*, 610–617.

Crockenberg, S. (1987). Predictors and correlates of anger toward and punitive control of toddlers by adolescent mothers. *Child Development, 58*, 964–975.

Denham, S. A., Bassett, H. H., & Wyatt, T. (2007). The socialization of emotional competence. In J. Grusec & P. Hastings (Eds.), *The handbook of socialization* (pp. 614–637). New York: Guilford Press.

Denham, S. A., Blair, K. A., DeMulder, E., Levitas, J., Sawyer, K., Auerbach-Major, S., & Queenan, P. (2003). Preschool emotional competence: Pathway to social competence? *Child Development, 74*, 238–256.

Denham, S. A., Mitchell-Copeland, J., Strandberg, K., Auerbach, S., & Blair, K. (1997). Parental contributions to preschoolers' emotional competence: Direct and indirect effects. *Motivation and Emotion, 21*, 65–86.

Eisenberg, N. (2000). Empathy and sympathy. In M. Lewis & J. M. Haviland (Eds.), *Handbook of emotions* (2nd Ed.) (pp. 677–691). New York: Guilford.

Eisenberg, N. Cumberland, A., & Spinrad, T. L. (1998). Parental socialization of emotion. *Psychological Inquiry, 9*, 241–273.

Eisenberg, N., & Fabes, R. A. (1994). Mothers' reactions to children's negative emotions: Relations to children's temperament and anger behavior. *Merrill-Palmer Quarterly, 40*, 138–156.

Feldman, R. (2003). Infant-mother and infant-father synchrony: The coregulation of positive arousal, *Infant Mental Health Journal, 24*, 1–23.

Fivush, R. (1989). Exploring sex differences in emotional content of mother-child conversations about the past. *Sex Roles, 20*, 675–691.

Fivush, R., Brotman, M. A., Buckner, J. P., & Goodman, S. H. (2000). Gender differences in parent-child emotion narratives. *Sex Roles, 42*, 233–253.

Halberstadt, A., Crisp, V. W., & Eaton, K. L. (1999). Family expressiveness: A retrospective and new directions for research. In P. Philippot & R. S. Feldman (Eds.), *Social context of nonverbal behavior* (pp. 109–155). New York: Cambridge University Press.

Izard, C. E., Youngstrom, E. A., Fine, S. E., Mostow, A. J., & Trentacosta, C. J. (2006). Emotions and developmental psychopathology. In W. Damon and R. Lerner (Series Eds.) & N. Eisenberg (Vol. Ed.), *Handbook of child psychology: Vol. 3. Social, emotional, and personality development* (6th ed., pp. 244–292). New York: Wiley.

Leaper, C. (2002). Parenting boys and girls. In M. Bornstein (Ed.), *Handbook of parenting: Vol. 1. Children and parenting.* New Jersey: Erlbaum.

Leaper, C., Anderson, K. J., & Sanders, P. (1998). Moderators of gender effects on parents' talk to their children: A meta-analysis. *Developmental Psychology, 34*, 3–27.

Lytton, H., & Romney, D. M. (1991). Parents' differential socialization of boys and girls: A meta-analysis. *Psychological Bulletin, 109*, 267–296.

Morris, A. S., Silk, J. S., Steinberg, L., Myers, S. S., & Robinson, L. R. (2007). The role of the family context in the development of emotion regulation. *Social Development, 16*, 361–388.

Rubin, K. H., Coplan, R. J., Fox, N. A., & Calkins, S. D. (1995). Emotionality, emotion regulation, and preschoolers' social adaptation. *Development and Psychopathology, 7*, 49–62.

Ruble, D. N., Martin, C. L., & Berenbaum, S. A. (2006). Gender development. In W. Damon & R. M. Lerner (Series Eds.) & N. Eisenberg (Vol. Ed.), *Handbook of child psychology: Vol. 3. Social, emotional, and personality development* (6th ed., pp. 858–932). New York: Wiley.

Saarni, C. (1985). Indirect processes in affect socialization. In M. Lewis & C. Saarni (Eds.), *The socialization of emotions* (pp. 187–209). New York: Plenum.

Schmidt, M. E., DeMulder, E. K., & Denham, S. A. (2002). Kindergarten social-emotional competence: Developmental predictors and psychosocial implications. *Early Child Development and Care, 172*, 451–462.

Serbin, L., Marchessault, K., McAffer, V., Peters, P., & Schwartzman, A. (1993). Patterns of social behavior on the playground in 9 to 11 year girls and boys: Relation to teacher perceptions and to peer ratings of aggression, withdrawal, and likability. In C. Hart (Ed.), *Children on playgrounds: Research perspectives and applications* (pp. 162–183). Albany: SUNY Press.

Siegel, S., & Alloy, L. (1990). Interpersonal perceptions and consequences of depressive-significant other relationships: A naturalistic study of college roommates. *Journal of Abnormal Psychology, 99*, 361–373.

Tenenbaum, H. R., & Leaper, C. (2002). Are parents' gender schemas related to their children's gender-related cognitions? A meta analysis. *Developmental Psychology, 38*, 615–630.

Thompson, R. A. (1994). Emotion regulation: A theme in search of definition. In N. A. Fox (Ed.), *The development of emotion regulation: Biological and behavioral Considerations* (pp. 25–52). United Kingdom: Blackwell.

NEW DIRECTIONS FOR CHILD and ADOLESCENT DEVELOPMENT • DOI: 10.1002/cd

Trentacosta, C. J., & Izard, C. E. (2007). Kindergarten children's emotional competence as a predictor of their academic competence in first grade. *Emotion, 7*, 77–88.

Tronick, E. Z., Cohn, J., & Shea, E. (1986). The transfer of affect between mothers and infants. In T. B. Brazelton & M. Yogman (Eds.), *Affective development in infancy* (pp. 11–25). Norwood, NJ: Ablex.

Underwood, M. K., Coie, J. D., & Herbsman, C. R. (1992). Display rules for anger and aggression in school-age children. *Child Development, 63*, 366–380.

Valiente, C., Fabes, R. A., Eisenberg, N., & Spinrad, T. L. (2004). The relations of parental expressivity and support to children's coping with daily stress. *Journal of Family Psychology, 18*, 97–106.

Zahn-Waxler, C. (2000). The development of empathy, guilt, and internalization of distress: Implications for gender differences in internalizing and externalizing problems. In R. Davidson (Ed.), *Anxiety, depression, and emotion.* (pp. 222–265). London: Oxford University Press.

AMY KENNEDY ROOT is an assistant professor of child development and family studies at West Virginia University. Her research interests include understanding how children's dispositional characteristics and caregiving experiences work together (or against one another) to impact children's socioemotional development throughout the early childhood years.

SUSANNE A. DENHAM is an applied developmental psychologist and professor of psychology at George Mason University. Her research focuses on children's social and emotional development. She is especially interested in the role of emotional competence in children's social and academic functioning. She is also investigating the development of forgiveness in children.

NEW DIRECTIONS FOR CHILD and ADOLESCENT DEVELOPMENT • DOI: 10.1002/cd

Chaplin, T. M., Casey, J., Sinha, R., & Mayes, L. C. (2010). Gender differences in caregiver emotion socialization of low-income toddlers. In A. Kennedy Root & S. Denham (Eds.), *The role of gender in the socialization of emotion: Key concepts and critical issues. New Directions for Child and Adolescent Development, 128,* 11–27. San Francisco: Jossey-Bass.

2

Gender Differences in Caregiver Emotion Socialization of Low-Income Toddlers

Tara M. Chaplin, James Casey, Rajita Sinha, Linda C. Mayes

Abstract

Low-income children are at elevated risk for emotion-related problems; however, little research has examined gender and emotion socialization in low-income families. The authors describe the ways in which emotion socialization may differ for low-income versus middle-income families. They also present empirical data on low-income caregivers' responses to their toddlers' emotion displays, with findings indicating more supportive and fewer punitive responses to boys' anger than to girls', but few gender differences for sadness/anxiety. Finally, they present two models (the emotion competence model and differential emotions model) for understanding relations between emotion socialization and the development of psychopathology, particularly in low-income children. © Wiley Periodicals, Inc.

S tudies have shown gender differences in children's emotion expression as early as preschool age, with girls showing greater sadness and anxiety/fear than boys and boys showing greater anger/aggression than girls, at least for middle-class children (Brody, 1999; Cole, 1986). These patterns of expression are consistent with gender roles in U.S. culture for females to be relationship-oriented and to show "softer" negative emotions and for males to be assertive and to more freely show anger (Brody & Hall, 2000; Jordan, Surrey, & Kaplan, 1991; Zahn-Waxler, Cole, & Barrett, 1991). But how do girls and boys come to internalize gender roles and to express different patterns of emotion? Emotional arousal and emotion expression have a basis in biology (Fox, 1994). However, boys' and girls' emotions may also be influenced by messages from their environment, including from caregivers (also referred to throughout as "parents").

As discussed in Chapter One of this volume, previous studies of parental socialization of emotion have shown gender differences, with girls receiving greater supportive responses for their sadness and anxiety and boys receiving greater support for their anger (e.g., Chaplin, Cole, & Zahn-Waxler, 2005; Fivush, 1989). Notably, these studies have examined emotion socialization processes mainly in Caucasian, middle-income families. The present chapter will discuss gender and emotion socialization in low-income families. It is important to understand emotion socialization in these families, given that they encounter multiple chronic stressors that impact child emotion and parent–child interactions. We will also describe potential consequences of gender differences in parental emotion socialization for children (and, in particular, low-income children): gendered socialization may lead boys and girls to adopt different patterns of emotion that may, in their extremes, contribute to risk for different types of psychopathology (Izard, 1972; Malatesta & Wilson, 1988).

In this chapter we focus on caregivers' responses to their children's emotions in low-income families, although "emotion socialization" also includes other aspects of family life, such as parents' own expressivity (Eisenberg, Cumberland, & Spinrad, 1998; Thompson & Meyer, 2007). Also, we focus on child gender differences, although differences between mothers and fathers in their socialization practices have also been found (see Kennedy Root and Denham, Chapter One) and are important to consider in low-income families.

Child Gender Differences in Parental Emotion Socialization in Middle-Class Families

Several studies have examined differences in parents' responses to girls' versus boys' emotions, with most research being on middle-class, Caucasian families. Findings from these studies are mixed, depending on whether the study examined general negative/positive emotion or discrete emotions (e.g., anger, sadness). Typically, studies that examined parents' responses to general emotions (or studies in which discrete emotions are combined into one category for analyses) found no differences in parents' response to boys' versus girls' emotions (questionnaire studies: Eisenberg & Fabes, 1994; Katz & Hunter, 2007; Roberts, 1999; Wong, Diener, & Isabella, 2008; except see Eisenberg, Fabes, & Murphy, 1996; observational studies: Lunkenheimer, Shields, & Cortina, 2007; Suveg, Zeman, Flannery-Schroeder, & Cassano, 2005). However, studies that examined parents' responses to specific emotions have found evidence that parents show more encouragement of girls' fear and sadness than boys' and of boys' anger than girls' (questionnaire studies: Birnbaum & Croll, 1984; Cassano, Perry-Parrish, & Zeman, 2007, Fuchs & Thelen, 1988; Klimes-Dougan et al., 2007; Zeman & Garber, 1996; observational studies: Adams, Kuebli, Boyle, & Fivush, 1995; Chaplin et al., 2005; Fivush, 1989; Fivush, Brotman, Buckner, & Goodman, 2000; Radke-Yarrow & Kochanska, 1990). These studies (as noted) differed in whether they used self-report or observational measures of emotion socialization. Both types of methods have strengths, with report studies revealing parent or child perceptions of socialization that cannot be observed, and observational studies showing parents' spontaneous responses to in-the-moment child emotion.

Child Gender Differences in Parental Emotion Socialization in Low-Income Families

An important consideration in research on child gender and emotion socialization is the role of socioeconomic status. It is important to determine whether the gender differences in emotion socialization found for (mostly Caucasian) middle-income families are also found for families from low-income environments (O'Neal & Magai, 2005). Children living in poverty are at elevated risk for difficulties in psychosocial, cognitive, and physical development (Brooks-Gunn & Duncan, 1997; Klerman, 1991). Low-income children show heightened levels of internalizing and externalizing behavior problems (Dodge, Pettit, & Bates, 1994; Linares et al., 2001; Qi & Kaiser, 2003), problems that are associated at least partially with emotional arousal and regulation. Poverty is also associated specifically with some aspects of emotion regulation, with low-income children showing problems with self-regulation and impulse control (Takeuchi, Williams, & Adair, 1991).

Parents living in poverty encounter significant and continuous economic and social stressors, such as inability to pay debts and difficulty meeting the family's material needs (Conger, Ge, Elder, Lorenz, & Simons, 1994). Perhaps due to increased stress, they have been found to show less responsive and more punitive parenting styles than middle-class parents

(McLoyd, 1990; Pinderhughes, Dodge, Bates, Pettit, & Zelli, 2000; Wood-worth, Belsky, & Crnic, 1996). Similarly, low-income parents may show unique types of emotion socialization behaviors (O'Neal & Magai, 2005). For example, a low-income parent may be too overwhelmed with life stressors to focus on encouraging or supporting a child's sadness or anxiety, emotions that do not present an immediate demand. Interestingly, O'Neal and Magai found, with a sample of inner-city low-income early adolescents, that youth perceived their parents as using more punishing responses with sadness than with other emotions. The authors interpreted this as parents' attempts to prepare the youth for their dangerous neighborhoods in which sadness displays would be a liability. Minimizing sadness may be adaptive for navigating inner-city environments. However, suppressing sadness may have drawbacks for youth in that sadness serves several positive functions, including eliciting sympathy from others (Izard & Ackerman, 2000).

It is important to note, also, that there is variability in parenting quality and emotion socialization among families living in poverty, with some parents discouraging emotion and some showing "supportive" emotion socialization responses. In fact, supportive emotion socialization behaviors (or other behaviors that encourage positive emotional development) may contribute to resilience in low-income children. For example, Garner found that low-income African American mothers observed matching and discussion of emotions was associated with more optimal child emotion regulation (Garner, 2006), whereas mothers' reported discouragement of emotion was associated with decreased knowledge of anger (but not fear or sadness) situations (Garner, Carlson Jones, & Miner, 1994). Further, O'Neal and Magai (2005) found that less reward of shame and greater matching of adolescents' anger by caregivers was related to greater teacher-reported externalizing problems in low-income African American and Caribbean American early adolescents.

Gender roles for emotion may also differ depending on socioeconomic context. For example, in working-class or low-income environments, girls may be socialized to appear "tough" to protect themselves and may thus not encounter socialization pressures to express softer emotions and avoid anger (Brown, 1998; Eisenberg, 1999; Miller & Sperry, 1987). In addition, different ethnic groups may have different display rules for emotion (and potentially for gender and emotion). For example, Matsumoto (1993) found that Caucasian adults rated displays of fear as more appropriate than Hispanic adults and sadness as more appropriate than African Americans and Asian Americans. This could mean, for example, that African American parents may discourage sadness in both boys and girls.

In terms of gender differences in emotion socialization, Garner's research on low-income African American families did not show gender differences in caregiver reports of their socialization of negative emotion (for example, Garner et al., 1994). However, this research examined negative emotion generally rather than separately for anger versus sadness/fear. O'Neal and Magai (2005) examined negative emotions separately in African American and Caribbean American early adolescents and found only one gender difference out of twenty comparisons—with girls reporting receiving more reward for shame than boys. Taken together, the research thus far suggests that gender differences in emotion socialization may be attenuated in low-income African American and/or Caribbean American families. However, these findings are limited to studies of parent and child reports of emotion socialization and so can only reflect the socialization practices for which parents and children are consciously aware (Fivush, 1998). It is important to complement such studies with observational studies of the in-the-moment emotion socialization in low-income families.

Study of Emotion Socialization in Low-Income Toddlers

Aims. In this study, we examined observed emotion socialization responses by low-income female caregivers to their toddlers' sadness/anxiety and anger displays. Our aim was to determine the extent to which gender differences in emotion socialization responses would be found in a low-income sample. We expected that caregivers might show more supportive and less-punishing responses to girls' sadness and anxiety than boys' and to boys' anger expressions than girls'. However, these gender differences might be smaller in our sample of low-income, primarily African American families.

Method. The sample was drawn from a larger study of prenatally cocaine-exposed and nonexposed children, all from low-income inner-city neighborhoods (see Mayes, Granger, Frank, Schottenfeld, & Bornstein, 1993 for a description of the sample). The present analyses focused on the nonexposed children. Sixty-five nonexposed children (33 boys, 32 girls) participated in a frustrating, toy wait task at age two-and-a-half years, with their primary caregivers present. Children were primarily African American (73%), with 15% Hispanic, and 8% Caucasian. All children had female caregivers, most of which were mothers (93%), with 2% aunts and 5% "other" female caregivers.

Toddlers were videotaped while participating in a toy wait task with the caregiver present. The toy wait task is a widely used task designed to elicit negative emotion in young children (for example, Cole, Teti, & Zahn-Waxler, 2003). In the task, the child is shown an attractive, new toy by a research assistant. The toy is then taken away and placed on a counter out of the child's reach. The child is instructed to wait six minutes for the toy and to instead play with other (less attractive) toys that are displayed on the floor.

Child emotion episodes were identified from the task, and based on facial, vocal, and postural cues were classified as either angry or sad/anxious (coding system based on Cole, Zahn-Waxler, & Smith, 1994). Sadness and anxiety were coded together because they have similar functions—that is, both promote withdrawal from situations and elicit sympathy from others (Izard & Ackerman, 2000). Eleven children displayed at least one episode of anger (range from one to five episodes), and 16 children displayed at least one sadness/anxiety episode (range from one to four episodes).

Caregiver responses to child emotion were coded using a system (Chaplin, 2008) based on existing emotion socialization questionnaires; primarily the Emotions as a Child (EAC) Socialization Scale (Magai, 1996), with an additional code for "caregiver distress" adapted from the Coping with Children's Negative Emotions Scale (CCNES; Fabes, Eisenberg, & Bernzweig, 1990). Coders rated caregiver responses in the ten seconds following the start time of each child emotion based on caregivers' verbalizations, behaviors, and/or emotion expressions. Caregiver responses were categorized as either *no response* or one or more of the following responses: *support/reward* (for example, affirming the emotion, hugging the child, rewarding/praising the child), *override* (dismissing the emotion or attempting to distract the child from the emotion/distress), *punish* (setting limits or otherwise punishing the child during the emotion episode, mocking the child), and *caregiver distress* (caregiver herself displaying negative emotion facially, vocally, and/or posturally, such as a harsh, angry tone of voice).

Results/Discussion

Child Emotion. We first analyzed gender differences in children's expressions of anger and sadness/anxiety, to see if differences found in Caucasian, middle-class families (with girls showing greater sadness/anxiety and less anger than boys) would also be found in this low-income primarily African American sample. We used t tests to compare boys' and girls' emotions. We did not find significant differences for sadness/anxiety (girls $M =.44$, $SD =.91$; boys $M =.55$, $SD =1.20$) or for anger (girls $M =.41$, $SD =1.01$; boys $M =.24$, $SD =.79$). In fact, the pattern of means suggests that girls actually showed slightly less sadness/anxiety and slightly greater anger than boys. A low sadness and high anger presentation may be more acceptable for girls in low-income urban areas, where girls' anger may help protect them in stressful, sometimes dangerous, neighborhoods (Miller and Sperry, 1987).

Caregiver Response Analyses. For caregiver response analyses, we only included those children ($n = 26$, 12 boys, 14 girls) who expressed one or more emotion in the task. These children were included because we were interested in caregivers' responses to children's emotions.

Although this is a small sample, this analysis is important in that it is one of few to examine observed emotion socialization in high-risk, low-income, primarily ethnic minority families.

Caregiver responses were divided by the number of child emotion expressions to control for child expressivity. Table 2.1 shows the percentages of caregiver responses to anger and sadness/anxiety for boys and girls. Differences between responses to boys versus girls were examined with t tests. There were no statistically significant gender differences, which is not surprising given the small sample size. However, below we present interesting descriptive statistics that suggest gender differences.

Anger. In response to anger, caregivers showed supportive reactions about seven times more often for boys than for girls (44% for boys, 6% for girls). Caregivers responded to anger with punishment about twice as often for girls than boys (38% for boys, 79% for girls). They responded with caregiver distress reactions about 6 times as often for girls than boys (6% for boys, 39% for girls). Override responses to child anger were more evenly distributed for boys versus girls (see Table 2.1).

These descriptive data suggest that these low-income, primarily African American caregivers respond in ways that encourage boys' anger and discourage/punish girls' anger. These gender differences are consistent with prior research on Caucasian middle-class families (for example, Chaplin et al., 2005), suggesting that low-income families may hold similar beliefs about girls' versus boys' anger despite the fact that anger may serve a function for girls in low-income neighborhood in terms of helping

Table 2.1. Mean Percentage of Caregiver Responses to Boys' and Girls' Anger and Sadness/Anxiety

	Boys (N = 12) Mean % (SD)	Girls (N = 14) M (SD)
Anger		
No response	6% (12.5)	0% (0)
Support	44% (51.5)	6% (15.1)
Override	38% (47.9)	36% (47.6)
Punish	38% (47.9)	79% (39.3)
Caregiver distress	6% (12.5)	39% (45.6)
Sadness/anxiety		
No response	28% (9.4)	9% (18.6)
Support	25% (37.7)	22% (41.1)
Override	31% (45.8)	50% (53.5)
Punish	25% (38.2)	31% (37.2)
Caregiver distress	0%	3% (8.8)

Note. Percentages do not total to 100 because mother responses could be double-coded.

them protect themselves from dangerous environments. Interestingly, caregivers also showed distress following girls' anger more than boys', suggesting that they were upset by girls' anger displays (perhaps because these displays are gender-role inconsistent).

Sadness/Anxiety. Caregiver responses to sadness/anxiety showed fewer consistent gender differences (see Table 2.1). Boys were more likely to receive no response to their sadness/anxiety than girls (28% for boys, 9% for girls), perhaps indicating that caregivers ignored boys' sadness/anxiety. This lack of reinforcement could lead boys to decrease sadness and anxiety expressions over time. For example, Chaplin and colleagues (2005) found that lower parent response to sadness/anxiety in preschoolers predicted children's lower expression of sadness/anxiety two years later.

Interestingly, there were no notable gender differences in supportive, punishing, or caregiver distress responses to sadness/anxiety. Regarding override responses, girls actually received somewhat greater override (dismissing) responses than boys (31% for boys, 50% for girls) for their sadness, which is different from research findings from middle-class families that girls' sadness/anxiety tend to be supported/rewarded more than boys'. In sum, caregivers showed few gender differences in response to child sadness/anxiety, and the gender differences that were found were mixed. Perhaps these mixed findings reflect different gender roles for sadness/anxiety in low-income minority families. These families may believe that softer negative emotions should be discouraged for both boys and girls. Future research could explore this possibility.

Limitations/Future Directions. The present study was limited by several factors. First, there was a low frequency of child emotion episodes. Thus, the findings are limited to children who were emotionally reactive to a toy being taken away. In observational studies, naturally occurring episodes of emotion do not always arise within the time period of observation. Future research should observe families across longer periods of time and multiple settings. Also, those children who displayed emotion in the task may be different from those who did not in terms of their temperament or their early caregiving history. Another limitation is that the study did not include male caregivers and therefore parent gender differences could not be examined herein. Additionally, the present study examined low-income, primarily African American inner-city toddlers. It is impossible to determine whether the pattern of results presented here are due to ethnicity, low-income status, or the inner-city environment. Future research should examine emotion socialization in larger samples of low-income families who differ by race and by neighborhood type (urban, rural). Despite these limitations, the study found interesting patterns of differential caregiver responses to anger and (to a lesser extent) sad/anxious emotion displays for boys versus girls in high-risk families.

Broader Implications of Gender Differences in Emotion Socialization for Child Adjustment

Given the patterns of gender differences in emotion socialization found in our study (and others), it is important to consider the implications of gender differences for children's social–emotional development. This is particularly important for low-income children, as these youth are at elevated risk for psychological problems, problems that often involve difficulties with emotion expression and regulation (Cicchetti & Cohen, 2006). In addition, low-income families often have more stressors (e.g., worries about paying bills, threats of being evicted, multiple residence changes, unsafe neighborhoods) and have fewer positive opportunities (e.g., access to good school systems and extracurricular activities) than middle-income families. Given the many stressors they must cope with on a day-to-day basis, low-income parents may show different emotion socialization behaviors than middle-income families, and these behaviors may have different consequences for children's development of psychopathology than they would for middle-income families.

Below we discuss the processes by which patterns of emotion socialization could contribute to the development of psychopathology in children and in low-income children in particular. There are at least two models describing this process, one that focuses on socialization of children's emotional competence generally and one that focuses on differential socialization of specific emotions as risk for specific forms of psychopathology.

Emotion Competence Model

First, in what we call the *emotion competence model*, it is proposed that parental responses that support child emotions, rather than punish or minimize emotions, lead to greater child emotional competence (Denham, 2007; Gottman, Katz, & Hooven, 1997). Emotional competence includes understanding one's own and others' emotions and expressing and regulating emotions in ways that are appropriate to the demands of a given context. A lack of emotional competence may lead to risk for psychological disorders. Thus, emotion socialization behaviors that foster emotional competence, such as "emotion coaching" (which involves the caregiver being aware of emotion, seeing emotional situations as opportunities for emotional closeness and teaching, listening to the child and validating his or her emotions, and helping the child find solutions to his or her problems) may decrease child psychopathology.

Children whose parents engage in emotion coaching or similar behaviors that support emotions show better emotional and social competence as compared to peers who are not emotion coached or supported. Emotion-coached preschoolers participate in less-negative play with friends, have better ability to focus their attention, and show less physiological indications of stress than their peers (Hooven, Gottman, & Katz, 1995). Mothers' supportive reactions (such as positive and nurturing reactions) to their preschoolers' displays of emotions were associated with children's better emotional competence (such as more optimal emotion regulation and reactions to peers' emotions) in a study of middle-class Caucasian families (Denham & Grout, 1993). In terms of psychological symptoms, mother's coaching responses to preschoolers' anger have been associated with lower teacher-rated internalizing symptoms and lower mother-rated total behavior problems in middle-class families (Hooven and others, 1995).

It is unclear whether low-income families engage in emotion coaching behaviors in the same way as middle-income families. Given the many stresses associated with low-income status, these parents may not have the energy or the resources to be able to respond to their children's emotions in validating ways at all times. Also, what may be "supportive" or optimal emotion socialization for low-income parents may look different than what is considered optimal in the context of Caucasian, middle-income families. For example, a parent living in a dangerous inner-city neighborhood who responds to their child's whimpering and crying by supporting the sadness ("it's okay to be sad") may not be adequately preparing the child for the neighborhood environment. This type of response to sadness may leave the child vulnerable to being the victim of bullying or violence, or to be less accepted by peers and other members of the community. For families in such neighborhoods, a more adaptive response might be to dismiss the sadness or to accept the sad feeling, but encourage suppression of sadness when in public. This discouragement of sadness might help the child to stay safe and develop close ties with peers—although it might also have costs for the child's ability to access and appropriately express sadness in non-dangerous situations.

There are few studies of low-income parents' emotion coaching-type responses to child emotion. Low-income mothers' supportive responses (matching the emotion and discussing emotion) have been associated with more constructive child emotion regulation, similar to middle-income families (Garner, 2006). Also, in one study, low-income parents' discouragement of negative emotion was associated with preschoolers' lower knowledge of angry situations (Garner et al., 1994). However, parents' discouragement of negative emotion was not linked to children's knowledge of sad or fearful situations, suggesting that emotion-coaching behaviors may have different consequences for low-income children's anger versus sadness/fear.

In sum, coaching of children's emotions, including sadness, anger, and positive emotions, can lead to emotional competence and a broad decreased risk for psychopathology in middle-income families and possibly also in low-income families. However, the emotion competence model does not provide an explanation for why some children who lack emotion coaching/support tend toward more externalizing psychopathology (such as oppositional defiant disorder), whereas others develop internalizing psychopathology (such as depression or anxiety disorders) (Zahn-Waxler, Klimes-Dougan, & Kendziora, 1998). The specificity of prediction is particularly important when considering child gender, as boys are more likely to develop externalizing problems in childhood and girls are more likely to exhibit depression and some forms of anxiety by adolescence (Achenbach, 1991; Hankin et al., 1998; Ollendick & Yule, 1990).

Differential Emotions Model

To develop a more specific predictive model, it may be useful to examine relations between parental responses to discrete emotions, such as anger and sadness, and the development of internalizing versus externalizing psychopathology (O'Neal and Magai, 2005). It has been theorized that encouragement/reward of particular emotions may lead children to express patterns of emotion that may, in conjunction with other risk factors, lead them toward particular forms of psychopathology (Chaplin & Cole, 2005; Izard, 1972; Malatesta & Wilson, 1988). Here we call this the *differential emotions model* (see O'Neal & Magai, 2005 for further discussion of this model). In this model, for example, parents' greater encouragement of sadness and anxiety in girls, if it is pervasive in the parenting style, may lead girls to develop a pattern of coping with difficult situations by focusing on sadness and anxiety. Over time and over a number of socialization experiences, if this pattern of emotion becomes too rigid, a girl may focus on sadness in most situations, even those in which anger/ assertiveness is the more appropriate response. This could, especially in the context of a stressful environment such as a low-income inner-city neighborhood, lead to greater use of passive, ruminative coping, exacerbated sad feelings, hopelessness, and possibly depression. In this way, selective socialization of sadness in girls may contribute to girls' greater rates of depression than boys' (see Fivush & Buckner, 1998; Keenan & Hipwell, 2005).

Interestingly, in low-income families and in some ethnic groups, sadness may be discouraged for both boys and girls. It would be interesting to examine whether gender differences in depression are attenuated in families that do discourage sadness equally for boys and girls.

Parents' greater encouragement of anger in boys may place boys at greater risk for developing externalizing behavior problems, problems that are characterized by angry and aggressive behavior. For example, parents who respond to a boy's angry outbursts by rewarding this anger, either with increased attention or with supportive responses, may contribute to an escalating cycle of more and more intense angry displays. These angry displays may be one factor contributing to the development of conduct problems (Cole, Michel, & Teti, 1994). It would be interesting to examine relations between gender, anger socialization, and the development of externalizing problems in low-income youth. It may be that anger is more acceptable in girls from low-income environments, leading girls to be at risk for externalizing behaviors, including high-risk behaviors like substance use and early sexual activity.

Potential Combined Model

Of course, not all children who show gender-role consistent emotion patterns will develop psychopathology; however, those children who have other risk factors (such as low socioeconomic status) may go down a trajectory that is influenced by relative encouragement of particular discrete emotions. Interestingly, it may be the combination of low emotion coaching (which may lead to a general lack of emotion competence) and attention to discrete emotions (which focuses a lack of competence on particular emotions) that together lead to psychopathology. So, for example, a parent who fails to discuss emotions may have a child who has less understanding of/appreciation for emotion. He or she may cope with negative feelings in inappropriate ways, such as sobbing uncontrollably or being physically aggressive when another child picks on him or her. If, in addition, this child's parent specifically punishes his or her sadness displays, the child may react to negative emotion by suppressing sad feelings and instead acting out in angry/aggressive ways. This could lead to later risk for the development of externalizing problems. Future research could empirically examine this combination of effects by examining both parental coaching responses and also parents' specific beliefs about or responses to particular discrete emotions. It may be particularly important to examine this in samples of low-income families, whose children are at high risk for the development of psychopathology and who may use different types of emotion socialization behaviors.

Conclusions/Future Directions

Taken together, our review of the literature and our findings with a sample of low-income, primarily African American toddlers suggests that there may be differences in parents' responses to girls' versus boys' emotions, although these may be attenuated in low-income and/or ethnic minority families. Gender differences in emotion socialization may be more evident when examining anger and sadness/anxiety separately because there are different gender stereotypes for these emotions, at least in dominant U.S. culture. Moreover, gender differences in parental responses to emotion are important in that they may contribute to gender differences in child emotion expression and psychopathology.

NEW DIRECTIONS FOR CHILD and ADOLESCENT DEVELOPMENT • DOI: 10.1002/cd

This chapter focused primarily on anger, sadness, and anxiety/fear. In addition to these emotions, future research should examine parental responses to other emotions, including joy, shame, and guilt. Shame and guilt, for example, may be more encouraged in girls than in boys and, if internalized to an excessive level, may lead them to develop depression (Zahn-Waxler et al., 1991). Also, of all the discrete emotions examined, only shame showed a gender difference in socialization in one sample of low-income inner-city youth, with girls reporting greater reward of their shame than boys (O'Neal & Magai, 2005).

In addition, longitudinal studies are needed to determine the consequences of emotion socialization for girls' and boys' social–emotional development over time. It would be of interest to examine this in at-risk families, for example in low-income families or in parents with psychopathology. Parents with depression, for example, may socialize (either through contingent responding or through modeling) a style of emotion regulation that involves coping with problems by ruminating on sadness. Finally, it would be of interest to examine interactions between biological markers of emotional reactivity (for example, heart rate, cortisol increases, activation of emotional centers of the brain, potential genetic markers) and parental emotion socialization to try to unravel the complex predictors of children's emotional competence, patterns of emotion, and subsequent psychological adjustment.

References

Achenbach, T. M. (1991). *Manual for the Child Behavior Checklist/4-18 and 1991 Profile*. Burlington: Department of Psychiatry, University of Vermont.

Adams, S, Kuebli, J., Boyle, P. A., & Fivush, R. (1995). Gender differences in parent-child conversations about past emotions: A longitudinal investigation. *Sex Roles, 33*(5–6), 309–323.

Birnbaum, D. W. & Croll, W. L. (1984). The etiology of children's stereotypes about sex differences in emotionality. *Sex Roles, 10*(9–10), 677–291.

Brody, L. R. (1999). *Gender, emotion, and the family*. Cambridge, MA: Harvard University Press.

Brody, L. R., & Hall, J. A. (2000). In M. Lewis & J. M. Haviland (Eds.), *Handbook of emotions*, (2nd ed., pp. 338-349). New York: The Guilford Press.

Brooks-Gunn, J. & Duncan, G. J. (1997). The effects of poverty on children and youth. *The Future of Children, 7*, 55–71.

Brown, L. M. (1998). *Raising their voices: The politics of girls' anger*. Cambridge, MA: Harvard University Press.

Cassano, M., Perry-Parrish, C., & Zeman, J. (2007). Influence of gender on parental socialization of children's sadness regulation. *Social Development, 16*(2), 210–231.

Chaplin, T. M. (2008). Emotion socialization observational coding system. Unpublished Manual. Yale University School of Medicine.

Chaplin, T. M., & Cole, P. M. (2005). The role of emotion regulation in the development of psychopathology. In B. L. Hankin & J. R. Z. Abela (Eds.), *Development of psychopathology: A vulnerability-stress perspective* (pp. 49–74). Thousand Oaks, CA: Sage.

Chaplin, T. M., Cole, P. M., & Zahn-Waxler, C. (2005). Parental socialization of emotion expression: Gender differences and relations to child adjustment. *Emotion, 5*, 80–88.

Cicchetti, D., & Cohen, D. J. (2006). *Developmental psychopathology: Theory and method*. Hoboken, NJ: John Wiley and Sons.

Cole, P. M. (1986). Children's spontaneous control of facial expression. *Child Development, 57*, 1309–1321.

Cole, P. M., Michel, M. K., & Teti, L. O. (1994). The development of emotion regulation and dysregulation: A clinical perspective. In N. A. Fox (Ed.), *The development of emotion regulation: Biological and behavioral considerations, Monographs of the Society for Research on Child Development 59* (2-3, Serial No. 240) 73–100.

Cole, P. M., Teti, L. O., & Zahn-Waxler, C. (2003). Mutual emotion regulation and the stability of conduct problems between preschool and early school age. *Development and Psychopathology, 15*, 1–18.

Cole, P. M., Zahn-Waxler, C., & Smith, K. D. (1994). Expressive control during a disappointment: Variations related to preschoolers' behavior problems. *Developmental Psychology, 30*, 835–846.

Conger, R. D., Ge, X., Elder, G. H., Lorenz, F. O., & Simons, R. L. (1994). Economic stress, coercive family process, and developmental problems of adolescents. *Child Development, 65*, 541–561.

Denham, S. A. (2007). Dealing with feelings: How children negotiate the worlds of emotions and social relationships. *Cognitie Creier Comportament, 11*(1), 1–48.

Denham, S. A., & Grout, L. (1993). Socialization of emotion: Pathway to preschoolers' emotional and social competence. *Journal of Nonverbal Behavior, 17*(3), 205–227.

Dodge, K. A., Pettit, G. S., & Bates, J. E. (1994). Socialization mediators of the relation between socioeconomic status and child conduct problems. *Child Development, 65*(2), 649–665.

Eisenberg, A. R. (1999). Emotion talk among Mexican American and Anglo American mothers and children from two social classes. *Merrill-Palmer Quarterly, 45*(2), 267–284.

Eisenberg, N., Cumberland, A., & Spinrad, T. L. (1998). Parental socialization of emotion. *Psychological Inquiry, 9*, 241–273.

Eisenberg, N., & Fabes, R. A. (1994). Mothers' reactions to children's negative emotions: Relations to children's temperament and anger behavior. *Merrill-Palmer Quarterly, 40*, 138–156.

Eisenberg, N., Fabes, R, A., & Murphy, B. C. (1996). Parents' reactions to children's negative emotions: Relations to children's social competence and comforting behavior. *Child Development, 67*, 2227–2247.

Fabes, R. A., Eisenberg, N., & Bernzweig, J. (1990). The Coping with Children's Negative Emotions Scale. Unpublished document available from the first author, Arizona State University, Tempe.

Fivush, R. (1989). Exploring sex differences in the emotional content of mother-child conversations about the past. *Sex Roles, 20*, 675–691.

Fivush, R. (1998). Methodological challenges in the study of emotional socialization. *Psychological Inquiry, 9*, 281–283.

Fivush, R., Brotman, M. A., Buckner, J. P., & Goodman, S. H. (2000). Gender differences in parent-child emotion narratives. *Sex Roles, 42*, 233–253.

Fivush, R., & Buckner, J. P. (1998). Gender, sadness, and depression: The development of emotional focus through gendered discourse. In A. H. Fisher (Ed.), *Gender and emotion: Social psychological perspectives* (pp. 232–253). New York: Cambridge University Press.

Fox, N. A. (1994). Dynamic cerebral processes underlying emotion regulation. *Monographs of the society for research in child development, 59*(2/3), 152–166.

Fuchs, D., & Thelen, M. H. (1988). Children's expected interpersonal consequences of communicating their affective state and reported likelihood of expression. *Child Development*, 59(5), 1314–1322.

Garner, P. W. (2006). Prediction of prosocial and emotional competence from maternal behavior in African American preschoolers. *Cultural Diversity and Ethnic Minority Psychology*, 12, 179–198.

Garner, P. W., Carlson Jones, D., & Miner, J. L. (1994). Social competence among low-income preschoolers: Emotion socialization practices and social cognitive correlates. *Child Development*, 65(2), 622–637.

Gottman, J., Katz, L. F., & Hooven, C. (1997). Meta-emotion: How families communicate emotionally. Hillsdale, NJ: Erlbaum.

Hankin, B. L., Abramson, L. Y., Moffitt, T. E., Silva, P. A., McGee, R., & Angell, K. (1998). Development of depression from preadolescence to young adulthood: Emerging gender differences in a 10-year longitudinal study. *Journal of Abnormal Psychology*, 107, 128–140.

Hooven, C., Gottman, J. M., & Katz, L. F. (1995). Parental meta-emotion structure predicts family and child outcomes. *Cognition and Emotion*, 9(2–3), 229–264.

Izard, C. E. (1972). *Patterns of emotions: A new analysis of anxiety and depression.* New York: Academic Press.

Izard, C.E., & Ackerman, B.P. (2000). Motivational, organizational, and regulatory functions of discrete emotions. In M. Lewis & J. M. Haviland (Eds.), *Handbook of emotions* (2nd ed., pp. 253–264). New York: The Guilford Press.

Jordan, J. V., Surrey, J. L., & Kaplan, A. G. (1991). Women and empathy: Implications for psychological development and psychotherapy. In J. V. Jordan, A. G. Kaplan, J. B. Miller, I. P. Stiver, & J. L. Surrey (Eds.), *Women's growth in connection: Writings from the Stone Center* (pp. 27–66). New York: The Guilford Press.

Katz, L. F., & Hunter, E. C. (2007). Maternal meta-emotion philosophy and adolescent depressive symptomatology. *Social Development*, 16(2), 343–360.

Keenan, K., & Hipwell, A. E. (2005). Preadolescent clues to understanding depression in girls. *Clinical Child and Family Psychology Review*, 8, 89–105.

Kennedy Root, A. (2010). The role of gender in the socialization of emotion: Key concepts and critical issues. In A. Kennedy Root and S. Denham (Eds.), *The role of gender in the socialization of emotion: Key concepts and critical issues. New Directions for Child and Adolescent Development*, 128, San Francisco: Jossey-Bass.

Klerman, L. V. (1991). *Alive and well?: Research and policy review of health programs for poor young children.* New York: National Center for Children in Poverty.

Klimes-Dougan, B., Brand, A. E., Zahn-Waxler, C., Usher, B., Hastings, P. D., Kendziora, K., & Garside, R. B. (2007). Parental emotion socialization in adolescence: Differences in sex, age and problem status. *Social Development*, 16(2), 326–342.

Linares, L. O., Heeren, T., Bronfman, E., Zuckerman, B., Augustyn, M., & Tronick, E. (2001). A mediational model for the impact of exposure to community violence on early child behavior problems. *Child Development*, 72, 639–652.

Lunkenheimer, E. S., Shields, A. M., & Cortina, K. S. (2007). Parental emotion coaching and dismissing in family interaction. *Social Development*, 16(2), 232–248.

Magai, C. (1996). Emotions as a child. Unpublished manuscript, Long Island University, Brooklyn.

Malatesta, C. Z., & Wilson, A. (1988). Emotion cognition interaction in personality development: A discrete emotions, functionalist analysis. *British Journal of Social Psychology*, 27, 91–112.

Matsumoto, D. (1993). Ethnic differences in affect intensity, emotion judgments, display rule attitudes, and self-reported emotional expression in an American sample. *Motivation and Emotion*, 17(2), 107–123.

Mayes, L. C., Granger, R. H., Frank, M. A., Schottenfeld, R., & Bornstein, M. H. (1993). Neurobehavioral profiles of neonates exposed to cocaine prenatally. *Pediatrics, 91,* 778–783.

McLoyd, V. C. (1990). The impact of economic hardship on black families and children: Psychological distress, parenting, and socioemotional development. *Child Development, 61,* 311-346.

Miller, P., & Sperry, L. L. (1987). The socialization of anger and aggression. *Merrill-Palmer Quarterly, 33*(1), 1–31.

Ollendick, T. H., & Yule, W. (1990). Depression in British and American children and its relation to anxiety and fear. *Journal of Consulting and Clinical Psychology, 58,* 126–129.

O'Neal, C. R., & Magai, C. (2005). Do parents respond in different ways when children feel different emotions? The emotional context of parenting. *Development and Psychopathology, 17,* 467–487.

Pinderhughes, E. E., Dodge, K. A., Bates, J. E., Pettit, G. S., & Zelli, A. (2000). Discipline responses: Influences of parents' socioeconomic status, ethnicity, beliefs about parenting, stress, and cognitive-emotional processes. *Journal of Family Psychology, 14,* 380–400.

Qi, C. H., & Kaiser, A. P. (2003). Behavior problems of preschool children from low-income families. *Topics in Early Childhood Special Education, 23*(4), 188–216.

Radke-Yarrow, M., & Kochanska, G. (1990). Anger in young children. In N. L. Stein, B. Leventhal, & T. Trabasso (Eds.), *Psychological and biological approaches to emotion* (pp. 297–310). Hillsdale, N.J.: Lawrence Erlbaum Associates, Inc.

Roberts, W. (1999). The socialization of emotional expression: Relations with prosocial behavior and competence in five samples. *Canadian Journal of Behavioral Science, 31,* 72–85.

Suveg, C., Zeman, J., Flannery-Schroeder, E., & Cassano, M. (2005). Emotion socialization in families of children with an anxiety disorder. *Journal of Abnormal Child Psychology, 33*(2), 145–155.

Takeuchi, D. T., Williams, D. R., & Adair, R. K. (1991). Economic stress in the family and children's emotional and behavior problems. *Journal of Marriage and the Family, 53,* 1031–1041.

Thompson. R. A., & Meyer, S. (2007). Socialization of emotion regulation in the family. In J. J. Gross (Ed.), *Handbook of emotion regulation* (pp. 249-268). New York: Guilford Press.

Wong, M. S., Diener, M. L., & Isabella, R. A. (2008). Parents' emotion related beliefs and behaviors and child grade: Associations with children's perceptions of peer competence. *Journal of Applied Developmental Psychology, 29,* 175–186.

Woodworth, S., Belsky, J. & Crnic, K. The determinants of fathering during the child's second and third years of life: A developmental analysis. *Journal of Marriage and Family, 58*(3), 679–692.

Zahn-Waxler, C., Cole, P. M., & Barrett, K. C. (1991). Guilt and empathy: Sex differences and implications for the development of depression. In J. Garber & K. A. Dodge (Eds.), *The development of emotion regulation and dysregulation* (pp. 243–272). Cambridge: Cambridge University Press.

Zahn-Waxler, C., Klimes-Dougan, B., & Kendziora, K. T. (1998). The study of emotion socialization: Conceptual, methodological, and developmental considerations. *Psychological Inquiry, 9*(4), 313–316.

Zeman, J., & Garber, J. (1996). Display rules for anger, sadness, and pain: It depends on who is watching. *Child Development, 67*(3), 957–73.

This work was supported by NIH grants K01-DA024759 (Chaplin) and R01-DA-06025 (Mayes).

TARA M. CHAPLIN is an assistant professor of psychiatry at the Yale University School of Medicine. Her research interests are in the role of gender and emotion regulation in the development of psychopathology in at-risk children and adolescents.

JAMES CASEY is a graduate student at UC Berkeley. His research interests include emotional mimicry and emotion regulation.

RAJITA SINHA is a professor of psychiatry and child study and the director of the Yale Stress Center (yalestress.org) at the Yale University School of Medicine. Her research interests include stress, emotion regulation, sex differences, impulse control, craving, and the development of addictive behaviors.

LINDA C. MAYES is the Arnold Gesell Professor of Child Psychiatry, Pediatrics, and Psychology at the Yale Child Study Center and special advisor to the dean of Yale University School of Medicine. Her research interests include emotional regulation in at-risk children and adolescents.

NEW DIRECTIONS FOR CHILD and ADOLESCENT DEVELOPMENT • DOI: 10.1002/cd

Denham, S. A., Bassett, H. Hamada, & Wyatt, T. M. (2010). Gender differences in the socialization of preschoolers' emotional competence. In A. Kennedy Root & S. Denham (Eds.), *The role of gender in the socialization of emotion: Key concepts and critical issues. New Directions for Child and Adolescent Development, 128*, 29–49. San Francisco: Jossey-Bass.

3

Gender Differences in the Socialization of Preschoolers' Emotional Competence

Susanne A. Denham, Hideko Hamada Bassett, Todd M. Wyatt

Abstract

Preschoolers' socialization of emotion and its contribution to emotional competence is likely to be highly gendered. In their work, the authors have found that mothers often take on the role of emotional gatekeeper in the family, and fathers act as loving playmates, but that parents' styles of socialization of emotion do not usually differ for sons and daughters. They also found several themes in the prediction of preschoolers' emotion knowledge and regulation. For example, sometimes mother–father differences in emotional style actually seem to promote such competence, and girls seem particularly susceptible to parental socialization of emotion. © Wiley Periodicals, Inc.

Preschool-aged children are increasingly required to meet self-regulatory and cognitive demands of preacademic learning. They also face many social hurdles entering the world of peers—communicating, expressing emotions in socially appropriate ways, reacting to difficult peers, building relationships. Emotional competence is vital in all these developmental tasks: Preschoolers who can regulate their expression and experience of various emotions are poised for far-reaching positive social, emotional, and academic outcomes (Cole, Teti, & Zahn-Waxler, 2003; Denham et al., 2003; Fantuzzo, Bulotsky-Shearer, Fusco, & McWayne, 2005; Miller et al., 2006; Trentacosta, Izard, Mostow, & Fine, 2006). Understanding their own and others' emotions also contributes strongly to their success.

Because emotional competence is so central to young children's success in many areas, we need to consider its promotion by important adults. It is the mission of this chapter, then, to examine more deeply the contributions of parental socialization to preschoolers' emotional competence. In particular, in concert with this volume's overarching topic, we focus on differences between and unique contributions of mothers and fathers. Although we are learning more and more about how parents' socialization of emotion generally promotes preschoolers' emotional competence, there is still much to learn about the crucial role of both parents' and children's gender (Brody, 1997; Brody & Hall, 1993).

Many factors help shape how mothers' and fathers' may differentially—at least some of the time—socialize emotions (see Chapter One). Following culturally approved gender roles, and operating in gender-specific contexts, mothers may be the carriers of the "emotional function" of the family, with fathers more likely filling playmate/disciplinarian roles (Bretherton, Lambert, & Golby, 2005; Garside & Klimes-Dougan, 2002; Lewis & Lamb, 2003). For example, we would expect mothers to express emotions that support relationship enhancement, such as shared joy, gratitude, and tenderness. In contrast, we would expect fathers to express more dominant emotions in service of assertive goals, such as anger (Chaplin, Cole, & Zahn-Waxler, 2005). Indeed, mothers are our "best bets" for shouldering the responsibility of the family's emotional gatekeeper. When compared to fathers, they are more intensely expressive of both positive and some negative emotions, more apt to experience a wider variety of emotions, and more accurate decoders of emotions. Such differences in emotions can really be considered gender roles.

Coupling these role expectations and functionally different emotional lives, we expect that mothers would indeed be very different socializers of emotions than fathers, with different contributions to their young children's emotional competence. At the same time, parents may socialize their sons' and daughters' emotional competence quite differently. For example, young boys and girls are encouraged to express the very gender-relevant emotions already noted for their mothers and fathers (Chaplin

NEW DIRECTIONS FOR CHILD and ADOLESCENT DEVELOPMENT • DOI: 10.1002/cd

et al., 2005; see also Chapter One). Complicating these already complex issues is the possibility that mothers and fathers may have their own ways to differentially socialize sons' and daughters' emotions. For example, fathers may respond particularly punitively to their sons' emotional outbursts, but not their daughters', with mothers treating their offspring more equally in this regard. Finally, mothers' and fathers' socialization of emotion may differentially contribute to children's emotional competence, and even these parent-specific contributions may be specific to sons or daughters. For example, if mothers do fill the role of family emotional gatekeeper, it could be that their teaching about emotions contributes more (or differently) to children's emotion knowledge than fathers'.

Following the central issues put forward in Chapter One, then, we focus in this chapter upon the role of fathers versus mothers in socializing their preschool-aged children's emotional competence. Knowing more about these differences and commonalities in mothers' and fathers' socialization, and about how these processes work together to promote positive outcomes, is crucial for both theoretical and applied considerations. For theory building we need to know two things. First, we need to know, do mothers' and fathers' means of socializing emotion differ according to dimensions explainable by existing gender theory? Second, we need to know whether each socialization factor, for each parent, adds to our ability to predict positive outcomes for young children. What aspects of socialization of emotion are most important, for which parent and which aspect of emotional competence? Does our theorizing "hold up" empirically? Applications of our findings could translate into parent training, tailored to mothers and fathers, to maximize children's emotional competence. Unique aspects of our chapter include our operationalization of socialization of emotion processes—we discuss the examination of both parents' observed and self-report emotional modeling, reactions to emotions, and teaching about emotions (Denham, Bassett, & Wyatt, 2007; Eisenberg, Cumberland, & Spinrad, 1998), and a comprehensive examination of emotional competence outcomes—that is both emotion knowledge and emotion regulation.

Socialization of Emotion

Current Framework and Findings. Parents loom large as omnipresent contributors to young children's emerging emotional competence (Eisenberg et al., 1998). In Chapter One we discuss some of these techniques, but more detail is useful here. First, parents exhibit (or model) a variety of emotions, which children observe. Children's emotions often require some kind of reaction from parents, as well. Finally, parents' intentional teaching about the world of emotions is an important area of socialization. Each of these mechanisms influences children's emotion

knowledge and emotion regulation. Based on theory and empirical findings, we consider socialization of emotion "best practices" to include
socializers' positive emotional expression and experience, accepting
and helpful reactions to preschoolers' emotions, and emphasis on teaching
about emotions, which in turn contribute to children's more sophisticated
emotional competence (for much more detail, see Denham, 2006;
Denham et al., 2007).

Parents' modeled emotions, whether relatively automatic or more
conscious, can contribute to children's understanding of emotions, either
via their specific profile of expressed emotions or their general affective
tone; positive expressiveness in the family promotes understanding of
emotions, perhaps because it renders children more open to learning and
problem solving (Fredrickson, 1998). Conversely, although exposure to
well-regulated negative emotion can be positively related to understanding of emotion (Garner, Jones, & Miner, 1994), exposure to parents' negative emotions often hampers young children's emotion knowledge,
perhaps via children's avoiding distressing emotional issues.

Although similar pathways between parents' emotions and young
children's emotion regulation can be envisioned, with children's observation of more positive emotion profiles serving as models for regulatory
processes, the literature on this aspect of socialization of emotional competence is scant. Moreover, viewing parental emotions is not the same as
seeing their emotion regulation in action.

Parents' supportive reactions to children's emotions (Eisenberg,
Fabes, & Murphy, 1996) may help the child in differentiating among
emotions (Denham & Kochanoff, 2002; Denham, Zoller, & Couchoud,
1994; Eisenberg et al., 2001; Fabes, Poulin, Eisenberg, & Madden-
Derdich, 2002). Such reactions may promote children's readiness to learn
about others' emotions, with more punitive or distressed reactions to children's emotions hampering their learning by rendering emotions a more
"taboo," sensitive, overly arousing topic. In the same vein, supportive
responses to children's emotions also are a supportive breeding ground for
emotion regulation (Denham, 1989; Denham & Grout, 1993; Eisenberg
et al., 2001).

In teaching about emotions, parents may draw attention to emotions
and validate or clarify the child's emotion, helping the child to express
emotions authentically, in a regulated manner. The scaffolded context
of chatting with a parent, especially mother, about emotional experience
helps the young child to formulate a coherent body of knowledge about
emotional expressions, situations, and causes (Denham & Kochanoff,
2002; Denham, Renwick-DeBardi, & Hewes, 1994; Denham et al., 1994;
Dunn, Brown, & Beardsall, 1991; Dunn, Brown, Slomkowski, Tesla,
& Youngblade, 1991; Dunn, Slomkowski, Donelan, & Herrera, 1995;
Racine, Carpendale, & Turnbull, 2007). Talk about emotions also gives
the child a new tool to use in the service of emotion regulation, allowing

them to separate impulses from behavior (Thompson, 1991), although the association between parental teaching and emotion regulation is understudied in families of preschoolers (see Shipman and others, 2007, for results with older children).

Gender-Related Findings. Thus, we are learning much about the ways in which parents socialize young children's emotional competence. However, examinations of gender-related issues surrounding this socialization and its contribution to preschoolers' emotional competence are much rarer. Some have been mentioned in Chapter One and elsewhere, but much more detail and interpretation regarding our population of interest—preschool-aged children—is warranted. What are the gender-differentiated findings about parents' modeling of, reactions to, and teaching about emotions?

Regarding modeling emotion, Garner and colleagues (Garner, Robertson, & Smith, 1997), for example, have found that mothers reported showing more positive emotion (especially to daughters) and more sadness around their children than fathers. Parents of sons, especially fathers, reported showing more anger. These findings echo our earlier theoretically based predictions. Moreover, fathers' positivity made an additional contribution, over and above mothers', to explained variance in children's ability to remain emotionally positive during a challenging peer play session; fathers' role as playmates may render their positivity important in partnership with mothers'.

Mothers are more supportive of, and fathers more punitive toward, their young children's emotions (Eisenberg et al., 1996; McElwain, Halberstadt, & Volling, 2007; Wong, McElwain, & Halberstadt, 2009). Eisenberg et al. (1996) also found that maternal, but not paternal, negative reactions to their gradeschoolers' emotions predicted the children's emotion regulation. Similarly, consistent with our "emotional gatekeeper" hypothesis, Denham and Kochanoff (2002) found that mothers' positive emotions and reactions to emotions predicted preschoolers' concurrent and later emotion knowledge much more often than fathers'. When fathers' concurrent positive emotions and reactions to child emotions did predict children's emotion knowledge, mothers' positive emotions and reactions made a *negative* contribution; it may be that children benefit when parents differ in their reactions to children's emotions (McElwain et al., 2007). In fact, children may learn much about emotions and their regulation when one parent or the other is more negatively expressive (within limits). We will return to both possibilities later.

Not all findings converge regarding parental differences in teaching about emotions, and fathers' emotion conversations are not as deeply studied as mothers'. Nonetheless, we can conclude that mothers talk more about emotions with their preschoolers than fathers do; parents talk more to daughters about emotions, especially specific ones such as sadness; and mothers and fathers sometimes differ in their emotion talk to sons and daughters (Adams, Kuebli, Boyle, & Fivush, 1995; Fivush, 1991; Fivush et al., 2003; Fivush, Brotman, Buckner, & Goodman, 2000; Kuebli, Butler, & Fivush, 1995). Mothers appear to stress the interpersonal nature of emotions (Fivush, 1991; Flannagan & Perese, 1998), and fathers sometimes appear not to view family conversations as opportunities to discuss emotions at all (Chance & Fiese, 1999). Finally, in Denham and Kochanoff (2002), mothers' teaching about emotion contributed to preschoolers' emotion knowledge, but fathers' emotion talk actually made a *negative* contribution—they talked more about emotions to those children who especially needed to regulate their emotions. This finding in particular reminds us of the specific roles we propose for mothers and fathers—with mothers teaching about emotions in a more narrative fashion, and fathers using emotion language to serve a more directive function.

Taken together, however, these findings only begin to flesh out answers to our gender-focused questions on how parents socialize emotion. Given the gendered world of emotion, we must examine systematically the questions put forward earlier, to consider the socializers and the socialized—mothers and fathers, girls and boys. It is clear from the state of our knowledge that more detail buttressed by solid methodology is required to promote empirical understanding of our theoretical problems set up here: How do preschoolers' fathers and mothers differ in all three aspects of socialization of emotion, both overall and for sons and daughters? How does their socialization of emotion contribute to both understanding and regulation as aspects of their children's emotional competence, as a whole and for boys and girls separately? To begin answering these questions, we turn to an illustrative study of socialization of preschoolers' emotional competence. Constructs assessed and analytical methodology follow directly from these questions.

Method

Participants and Procedures. We worked with 80 preschoolers and their parents (48 boys; 53 followed from age 3 through kindergarten, mostly upper-middle class Caucasians). Children were between 3 and 4 years old when their families were visited. During the home visit, we studied self-reports and observations of all three aspects of socialization of emotions already outlined here: parental expressiveness, reactions to children's emotions, and teaching about emotions. Understanding and regulation of emotions were assessed when children were 3 to 4 years old and in kindergarten. Outcome and predictor measures are summarized for the reader in Table 3.1 and discussed briefly here. For all measures, psychometric properties were good to excellent.

NEW DIRECTIONS FOR CHILD and ADOLESCENT DEVELOPMENT • DOI: 10.1002/cd

Table 3.1. Summary of Predictor and Outcome Measures

Predictors and outcomes	Method/operationalization
Parent Measures—Predictors	
Observed expressive balance	Observation of emotional expressions: Prevalence of happiness minus prevalence of sadness, anger, and fear
Self-reported expressive balance	Self-Expressiveness Within The Family Questionnaire: Positive minus negative expressiveness scores
Observed parental reactions to emotions balance	Observation of reactions to children's emotional expressions: Standard scores for positive matching, positive reinforcing, and prosocial reactions minus standard scores for rates of antisocial and passive reactions were subtracted.
Self-reported parental reactions to emotions balance	Coping with Children's Negative Emotions Scale: Coaching totals (emotion- or problem-focused coping, and encouraging emotions) minus dismissing totals (punitive, minimizing, and distress reactions)
Observed parental teaching about emotions	Conversations about emotional events: Sum of parents' positive and negative emotion terms
Self-reported parental teaching about emotions	Emotion-Related Beliefs Scale: Summed items as an index of parents' valuing teaching their children about emotions
	Parent-rated parent inductive discipline: Average induction score, summing the continuum level of each response, and dividing by the number of responses given
Child Measures—Outcomes	
Emotion Knowledge Aggregate, Ages three to four	Sum of standard scores for receptive and expressive identification, and two emotion situation tasks
Display rule knowledge, kindergarten	Total score for understanding display rules (hiding + showing)
Constructive, venting, and avoidant coping	Sum of parent-report items

Measures of Socialization of Emotion: Parental Expressiveness

Observation of Emotional Expressions. Parents' emotions and reactions to the child's emotions were observed for a total of ninety minutes during home visits. Parents' observed expressive balance score was created by subtracting the percentage of angry, sad, and fearful displays from the percentage of happy displays.

Self-Expressiveness Within the Family Questionnaire. On an adaptation of the Family Expressiveness Questionnaire (SEFQ: Halberstadt et al.,

1995), parents reported their frequency of emotional displays within their family. For each parent, a self-reported expressive balance score equaled the difference between positive and negative expressiveness scores.

Measures of Socialization of Emotion: Reactions to Children's Emotions

Observed Reactions to Children's Emotions. Reactions to emotions were observed during the home visit. For the observed reactions to emotions balance score, standard scores for rates of antisocial and passive reactions were subtracted from the sum of standard scores for rates of positive matching, positive reinforcing, and prosocial reactions.

Coping with Children's Negative Emotions Scale. In the Coping with Children's Negative Emotion Scale (CCNES: Fabes, Poulin, Eisenberg, & Madden-Derdich, 2002), parents rated how likely they are to choose reactions to specific scenarios involving children's negative emotions. Balance scores for self-reported reactions to emotions equaled the difference between coaching totals (emotion- or problem-focused coping, and encouraging emotions responses) and dismissing totals (punitive, minimizing, and distress reaction responses).

Measures of Socialization of Emotion: Coaching About Emotions

Conversations About Emotional Events. Each parent–child dyad performed a semi-structured naturalistic task to assess emotion language; they reminisced about times when each of them had shown happy, sad, angry, and afraid emotions in the other's presence. The audiotaped, transcribed conversations were coded using the Parent-Child Affect Communication Task (PACT) System (Denham et al., 1994). For this study, parents' positive and negative emotion terms, as well as total references to self, target, and others, were summed.

Emotion-Related Beliefs Scale. Hyson and Lee's (1996) Teacher Emotion-Related Beliefs (ERB) measure was adapted for parents. Sample items include "I spend a lot of time talking to my children about why they feel the way they do." Items were summed to create an index of parents' valuing teaching their children about emotions.

Measures of Children's Emotional Competence

Children's Coping with Negative Emotion. Eisenberg and colleagues' (Eisenberg et al., 1993) Children's Coping with Negative Emotion Questionnaire, was used to measure children's emotion regulation. Mothers (when children were 3 to 4 years old) and kindergarten teachers rated the likelihood that the child would engage in constructive, emotional venting, and avoidant coping emotion regulatory responses (Eisenberg & Fabes, 1994).

Emotion Knowledge (3- to 4-Year-Old Assessment): Affect Knowledge Test (AKT). Because these measures have been described in detail elsewhere (Denham and Couchoud, 1990a, 1990b), they are summarized as follows: Children receptively and expressively identified happy, sad, angry, and afraid facial expressions drawn on flannel faces. For emotionally unequivocal and equivocal situation identification tasks, a puppeteer made standard facial and vocal expressions of emotions while enacting an emotion-laden story. The child was asked to place, on the puppet, the flannel face depicting the puppet's feeling in the situation. Standard scores for each item of these tasks were summed for the emotion knowledge aggregate.

Kindergarten Assessment Test: Knowledge of Emotion Display Rules (Gross and Harris, 1988). In each of six stories, a feeling needed to be hidden or shown (in a "hiding" story, protagonists need to hide sadness to avoid big brother's teasing; in a "showing" story, sadness needed to be shown when lost in a store and needing help). We used a total score for understanding display rules.

Results and Discussion

Socialization of Emotion: Mother/Father Differences, Child Gender Differences, and Interactions Between Parenting and Child Gender. How do we understand the impact of gender on the emotional lives of families? How can we describe the experience of little girls and boys, fathers and mothers? We first asked whether mothers and fathers differed in their observed and self-reported expressiveness balance, whether there were overall child gender differences in how parents socialized emotional competence, and, finally, whether parent effects were moderated by child gender. Results are shown in Table 3.2.

Many interpretable differences in socialization of emotion were found based on parent gender. Fathers' observed expressive balance was greater than mothers'. In contrast, mothers self-reported expressive balance score was greater than fathers'. This dichotomy at first seemed puzzling, but then we realized that fathers, as playmates, may indeed show more happiness than mothers (the only positive emotion we observed); in contrast, mothers were able to report on a range of positive and negative emotions on the SEFQ; this self-report also fits with Brody and Hall's (1993) review of female expressiveness.

Regarding differences in mothers' and fathers' reactions to children's emotions, mothers reported significantly more positive reactions, relative to negative ones, than fathers. There were no significant effects for observed reactions to emotions (see also Cassano, Perry-Parrish, & Zeman, 2007). Moreover, for both expressiveness and reactions to emotions, there were no significant main effects or interactions involving child gender. Regarding the seeming inconsistency between observational and self-report methodologies, parents may be able to envision a wider variety of child emotions to react to than we were able to observe during the home visits.

For observed conversations about emotions, fathers talked more about emotions to daughters than to sons. These findings with fathers

Table 3.2. Socialization of Emotion Differences: Parent, Child Gender, and Parent × Child Gender Effects

	F Parent	F Child gender	F Parent × child gender	Other
Observed expressive balance	4.69* Fathers more positive	—		
Self-reported expressive balance	7.46** Mothers more positive	—		
Observed parental reactions to emotions balance		—		
Self-reported parental reactions balance	89.1*** Mothers more positive	2.67+ More positive to boys	—	
Observed parental teaching about emotions		—	4.68* Fathers talk more to girls	○ Parent × Valence × Child Gender $F = 4.66*$ ○ Mothers talk more than fathers, to sons, about negative emotions ○ Parent × Valence × Referent = 13.01*** ○ Mothers talk more about self-emotions than fathers
Self-reported parental teaching about emotions	20.93*** Mothers higher on PDS 61.73*** Mothers higher on ERB	—	—	

Note. + $p < .10$, * $p < .05$, ** $p < .01$, *** $p < .001$.
ERB = Emotion-Related Beliefs Scale. PDS = Parent Disciplinary

echo those that Adams and colleagues (1995; see also Kuebli & Fivush, 1992) found for both parents. In our study, however, in contrast to Fivush and colleagues (2003; see also Fivush, 1991), mothers talked about emotions equivalently to boys as to girls, but talked far more to sons about negative emotions than did fathers. Moreover, mothers talked more about their own negative emotions than did fathers, with fathers talking more about the child's and other persons' emotions. Finally, mothers reported valuing teaching about emotions, more than fathers. Many of these differences would be predicted by gender theory; we see the difference in mothers' talk about their own emotions as parallel their greater focus on the interpersonal in discussions of emotion with their young children (Chance & Fiese, 1999; Fivush et al., 2000).

Thus, our findings tell us that mothers and fathers do socialize preschoolers' emotional competence differently. However, parents' emotion socialization of boys and girls generally did not differ (see also Klimes-Dougan et al., 2007, for similar findings). Further, Parent × Child Gender interactions only appeared for conversations about emotion. Thus, we see a nuanced picture of mothers' and fathers' affective environment provided to preschoolers, in which mothers appeared to bear the responsibility for the emotional function of the family. At the same time, though, fathers' roles as enthusiastic, emotionally positive playmates and their discussions of emotions with daughters came to light.

Predicting Emotional Competence. Next, we asked how maternal and paternal aspects of socialization of emotions uniquely predicted aspects of preschoolers' emotional competences, and whether such prediction varied for boys and girls. We accomplished this goal via a series of multiple regression equations. Criterion variables were preschool and kindergarten aspects of emotional competence. In the first step of separate equations, we entered mothers' and fathers' observed and self-reported indices for each socialization factor and child's gender. The results of the first step of regressions are summarized in Table 3.3 (for simplicity, only beta weights for borderline or significant predictors are shown).

Next, because one of our foci was on child gender's effects on the relation between parental socialization of emotion and child outcome, we created interaction terms between child's gender and each socialization factor, and entered these in a second step. We interpret only those where post hoc probing (Holmbeck, 2002) indicated significant betas for boys or girls; Figures 3.1 through 3.7 show the results of these post hoc probings.

Children's Emotion Knowledge. Mother's observed expressive balance *negatively* and fathers' observed expressive balance and self-reported expressive balance *positively* predicted preschool emotion knowledge. Maternal self-reported expressive balance negatively predicted kindergarteners' later display rule knowledge, especially girls' (see Figure 3.1), whereas paternal self-reported expressive balance *positively* predicted

Table 3.3. Socialization of Emotion's Contribution to Preschoolers' Emotion Knowledge and Emotion Regulation at Ages 3 to 4 and in Kindergarten

Child outcomes	Observed parental	Self-reported parental
	Parental expressive balance	
Emotion knowledge aggregate, ages 3 to 4	$\beta_{Mother} = -.312^*$ $\beta_{Father} = .368^{**}$	$\beta_{Father} = .204^+$
Display rule knowledge, kindergarten	—	$\beta_{Mother} = -.460^{**}$ $\beta_{Father} = .319^{**}$
Avoidant coping, ages 3 to 4	$\beta_{Mother} = -.262^+$	—
Avoidant coping, kindergarten	$\beta_{Mother} = .306^+$	$\beta_{Father} = .293^+$
	Parental reactions to emotions balance	
Constructive coping, ages 3 to 4	—	$\beta_{Mother} = .298^*$
Avoidant coping, ages 3 to 4	$\beta_{Mother} = -.224^+$	$\beta_{Mother} = .201^+$
Constructive coping, kindergarten	$\beta_{Father} = .234^+$	—
Venting coping, kindergarten	$\beta_{Mother} = -.358^+$ $\beta_{Father} = .317^*$	—
	Parental teaching	
Display rule knowledge, kindergarten	$\beta_{Mother\ Positive} = -.343^+$ $\beta_{Mother\ Negative} = .402^*$	—

Note. $^+p < .10$, $^*p < .05$, $^{**}p < .01$.

Figure 3.1. Mothers' Self-Reported Expressive Balance Predicting Display Rule Knowledge for Kindergarten Boys and Girls

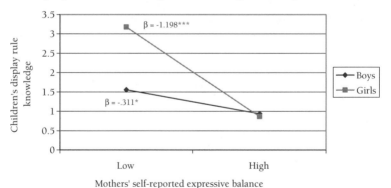

the same index, again especially for girls (see Figure 3.2). Thus, parental patterns of expressiveness also worked together in interesting ways. Perhaps viewing this mixed emotionality gives children a window into the complexity of the full range of emotions, especially the need for display rules (McElwain, Halberstadt, & Volling, 2007). Further, it may be that fathers' showing and/or reporting more positive emotions allowed for children's secure emotional foundation, and the mildly negative emotions reported by or seen in mothers afforded children the exposure necessary to acquire rich emotion knowledge.

Finally, maternal usage of positive emotion terms *negatively*, and maternal usage of negative emotion terms *positively* predicted, kindergartners' later display rule knowledge. Perhaps knowing more about negative emotions is more germane to learning which emotions should be expressed and which hidden. In sum, mothers' fuller, gender-expected, display of and teaching about negative emotions, and their contribution to children's emotion knowledge, may be part of their emotional gatekeeper role in the family.

Another theme in our findings is that of "missing socialization factors"—for example, parental reactions to children's emotions did not predict emotion knowledge, in contrast with earlier research, such as both Denham and others (1994) and Fabes and others (2002). It may be that methodological and analytical decisions in this study rendered any possible contributions of parental reactions to emotions to emotion knowledge harder to discern.

Emotion Regulation. Differences between what parents say and what observers see, which may be more content than methodology, constitute another theme in our regression findings. For example, where mothers were observed to show more negative emotions, but reported a positive emotional substrate in the family, preschool-aged daughters evidenced more constructive emotion regulatory strategies (see Figures 3.3 and 3.4). As with display rule knowledge, perhaps this mixture of emotional events gives children, particularly daughters, fodder to construct workable emotion regulatory coping strategies

At the same time, maternal observed expressive balance negatively predicted preschoolers' avoidant emotion regulation strategies; in

Figure 3.2. Fathers' Self-Reported Expressive Balance Predicting Display Rule Knowledge for Kindergarten Boys and Girls

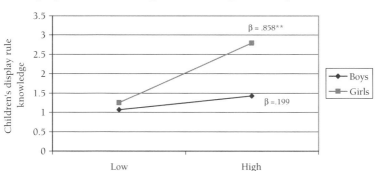

Figure 3.3. Mothers' Observed Expressive Balance Predicting Constructive Coping for Preschool Boys and Girls

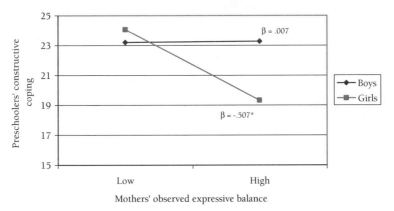

Mothers' observed expressive balance

Figure 3.4. Mothers' Self-Reported Expressive Balance Predicting Constructive Coping for Preschool Boys and Girls

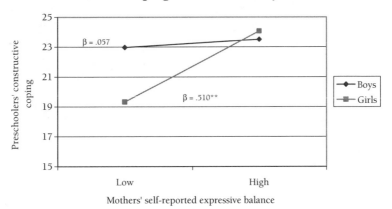

Mothers' self-reported expressive balance

contrast, it positively predicted kindergartners' use of avoidant emotion regulation strategies, as did fathers' self-reported expressive balance. These findings are difficult to reconcile, but perhaps the profile of more avoidant emotion regulatory strategies (for example, distraction, leaving, ignoring the situation) changes across the two-year-period of study. For 3-year-olds, maternal negativity may promote children's use of leaving when faced with emotionally difficult situations—that is, the children want to escape mothers' and their own negative feelings. In contrast, by the time children are mature kindergartners, their parents' positive emotional styles may have formed a foundation for the use of distraction to maintain an even kool.

NEW DIRECTIONS FOR CHILD and ADOLESCENT DEVELOPMENT • DOI: 10.1002/cd

For parents' reactions to children's emotions, preschoolers' constructive emotion regulation strategies were predicted at a borderline level of significance by mothers' self-reported reactions to emotions balance. Kindergartners', especially boys' (see Figure 3.5), constructive emotion regulation strategies were predicted by fathers' observed reaction balance two years earlier. Thus, mothers' and fathers' optimal reaction patterns are useful at different time periods and, at least for fathers, more so for same-sex pairings. These patterns of prediction need replication and their theoretical underpinnings need further consideration. It seems logical, however, that parents' more supportive reactions to children's emotions could serve as models of constructive emotion regulation, as well as allowing for more "teachable moments" about emotions.

Preschoolers' avoidant emotion regulation strategies were negatively predicted at a borderline level of significance by mothers' observed reaction balance, but *positively* predicted by mothers' self-reported reactions to emotions balance score. Venting emotion regulation strategies in kindergarten were *negatively* predicted by mothers' observed reaction balance, but *positively* by fathers' observed reaction balance. Here we again see both themes of differential prediction by mothers and fathers and from differing methodologies.

Regarding parental teaching about emotions, where mothers talked more about positive emotion, their preschool-aged sons less frequently used venting emotion regulation strategies, and their daughters less frequently used avoidant emotion regulation strategies (see Figures 3.6 and 3.7). The greater salience of the family context for girls' behavior here and in earlier findings is worthy of note (see also Denham et al., 1997). Both aspects of girls' emotional competence, during at least one age period, were particularly susceptible to parental socialization of emotion and its distinctions.

Figure 3.5. Fathers' Self-Reported Reactions to Emotions Balance Predicting Kindergartners' Constructive Coping for Boys and Girls

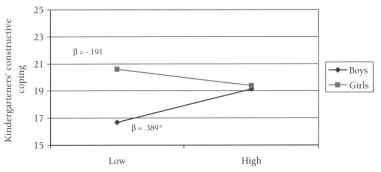

Figure 3.6. Mothers' Usage of Positive Emotion Terms Predicting Venting Coping for Preschool Boys and Girls

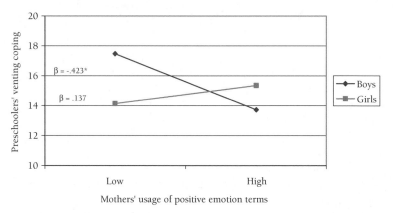

β = -.423*

β = .137

Mothers' usage of positive emotion terms

Figure 3.7. Mothers' Self-Reported Expressive Balance Predicting Display Rule Knowledge for Kindergarten Boys and Girls

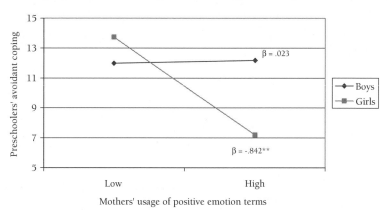

β = .023

β = -.842**

Mothers' usage of positive emotion terms

Daughters seem to be quintessential observers of parents' emotions and listeners to parents' teaching about emotions.

However, returning to the notion of "missing socialization factors," there were few contributions of parental teaching to children's emotion regulation strategies. As noted earlier, this theoretically appealing notion has not been tested. It may be that children's regulatory strategies are still intimately tied to their more biologically based temperamental reactivity at this point (Rothbart, Posner, & Kieras, 2006), and as yet less amenable to parental teaching. In any case, little regulation-related emotion language from either parent was seen in these data. Less-reactive youngsters may be more easily socialized at this age (Mirabile, Scaramella, Sohr-Preston, & Robison, 2009); in future studies such moderation should be more extensively studied.

Finally, it is clear that inclusion of paternal report and observations of fathers were important in fleshing out the entire picture of socialization of emotion during the preschool years. Fathers' socialization figured in emotion knowledge, as well as all three emotion regulatory strategies. Studying only maternal socialization of emotion would, then, leave us with incomplete understanding of the socialization of young children's emotional competence.

Conclusion

In sum, we found that parents of preschoolers do differ in their socialization of emotion, but that mothers' and fathers' styles do not usually differ for sons and daughters (except where conversing about emotions). We also found several themes in the prediction of preschoolers' emotion knowledge and regulation. Mothers' and fathers' socialization of emotion styles are different in predictable ways—with mothers as emotional gatekeeper and fathers as loving playmate. As well, their techniques differentially predict young children's emotional competence, and sometimes mother–father differences in emotional style actually seem to promote such competence. Girls seem particularly susceptible to parental socialization of emotion. Finally, sometimes differences between what parents said and what observers saw seemed interpretable, rather than mere methodological error, and some socialization factors did not predict either emotion knowledge or emotion regulation.

Where do we (and others) go from here? How do these results challenge our thinking or point to a new direction in this field? First, several of the themes require more attention—for example, those about differences in parental predictors and methodologies could be profitably explored further. The issue of children making use of emotional divergences in their parents is an intriguing one brought up by McElwain et al. (2007), and it seems ready for deeper investigation. Second, our findings about girls should be integrated into the larger literature on development of girls' social-emotional competence and psychopathology (Zahn-Waxler, Shirtcliff, & Marceau, 2008). Third, our findings on mothers as bearing the family's emotional function (with fathers as support figures) during the preschool period fit well with other literature in the area, and point to a new direction: It would be useful to move away from our focus on the preschool period, to examine these specific aspects of parental socialization of emotion and emotional competence sequelae through adolescence. For example, it could be conjectured that parents' socialization of emotion might become more restrictive as children age, and that certain differences between parents and in ways of treating boys and girls might diminish or intensify (just how is an empirical question, and ripe for more pinpointed theorizing).

Finally, future work needs to be done with samples composed of other cultural or socioeconomic groups, for whom socialization of emotion and its relation to gender may have different meanings. Other clinical subsamples, such as families where there is interparental conflict, even violence, or maternal depression, should be studied in this regard, as well.

In short, our findings confirm the importance of the inclusion of data from both parents, considering the function of emotions within the family, and taking into account parent and child gender when fleshing out the entire picture of socialization of emotional competence during the preschool years. It is hoped that these results and accompanying thinking will spur the field to greater study and understanding of these issues.

References

Adams, S., Kuebli, J., Boyle, P. A., & Fivush, R. (1995). Gender differences in parent-child conversations about past emotions: A longitudinal investigation. *Sex Roles*, *33*(5), 309–323.

Bretherton, I., Lambert, J. D., & Golby, B. (2005). Involved fathers of preschool children as seen by themselves and their wives: Accounts of attachment, socialization, and companionship. *Attachment & Human Development*, *7*(3), 229–251.

Brody, L. R. (1997). Gender and emotion: beyond stereotypes. *Journal of Social Issues*, 1997, *53*(2), 369–393.

Brody, L. R., & Hall, J. A. (1993). Gender and emotion. In M. Lewis & J. M. Haviland (Eds.), *Handbook of emotions*. New York: Guilford Press.

Cassano, M., Perry-Parrish, C., & Zeman, J. (2007). Influence of gender on parental socialization of children's sadness regulation. *Social Development*, *16*(2), 210–231.

Chance, C., & Fiese, B. H. (1999). Gender-stereotyped lessons about emotion in family narratives. *Narrative Inquiry*, *9*(2), 243–255.

Chaplin, T. M., Cole, P. M., & Zahn-Waxler, C. (2005). Parental socialization of emotion expression: Gender differences and relations to child adjustment." *Emotion*, *5*(1), 80–88.

Cole, P. M., Teti, L. O., & Zahn-Waxler, C. (2003). Mutual emotion regulation and the stability of conduct problems between preschool and early school age. *Development and Psychopathology*, *15*(1), 1–18.

Denham, S. A. (1989). Maternal affect and toddlers' social-emotional competence. *American Journal of Orthopsychiatry*, *59*(3), 368–376.

Denham, S. A. (2006). Emotional competence in preschoolers: Implications for social functioning. In J. Luby (ed.), *Handbook of preschool mental health: Development, disorders and treatment*. New York: Guilford.

Denham, S. A., Bassett, H. H., & Wyatt, T. (2007). The socialization of emotional competence. In J. Grusec and P. Hastings (Eds.), *The handbook of socialization*. New York: Guilford Press.

Denham, S. A., Blair, K. A., DeMulder, E., Levitas, J., Sawyer, K., Auerbach-Major, S, & Queenan, P. (2003). Preschoolers' emotional competence: Pathway to mental health? *Child Development*, *74*(1), 238–256.

Denham, S. A., & Couchoud, E. A. (1990a). Young preschoolers' understanding of emotion. *Child Study Journal*, *20*(3), 171–192.

Denham, S. A., & Couchoud, E. A. (1990b). Young preschoolers' understanding of equivocal emotion situations. *Child Study Journal, 20*(3), 193–202.

Denham, S. A., & Grout, L. (1993). Socialization of emotion: Pathway to preschoolers' emotional and social competence. *Journal of Nonverbal Behavior, 17*(3), 205–227.

Denham, S. A., & Kochanoff, A. T. (2002). Parental contributions to preschoolers' understanding of emotion. *Marriage & Family Review, 34*(3/4), 311–343.

Denham, S. A., Renwick-DeBardi, S., & Hewes, S. (1994). Emotional communication between mothers and preschoolers: Relations with emotional competence. *Merrill-Palmer Quarterly, 40*(4), 488–508.

Denham, S. A., Zoller, D., & Couchoud, E. A. (1994). Socialization of preschoolers' emotion understanding. *Developmental Psychology, 30*(6), 928–936.

Dunn, J., Brown, J. R., & Beardsall, L. A. (1991). Family talk about emotions, and children's later understanding of others' emotions. *Developmental Psychology, 27*(3), 448–455.

Dunn, J., Brown, J. R., Slomkowski, C., Tesla, C., & Youngblade, L. (1991). Young children's understanding of other people's feelings and beliefs: Individual differences and their antecedents. *Child Development, 62*(6), 1352–1366.

Dunn, J., Slomkowski, C., Donelan, N., & Herrera, C. (1995). Conflict, understanding, and relationships: Developments and differences in the preschool years." *Early Education and Development, 6*(4), 303–316.

Eisenberg, N., Cumberland, A. J., & Spinrad, T. L.(1998). Parental socialization of emotion. *Psychological Inquiry, 9*(4), 241–273.

Eisenberg, N., Fabes, R. A., Bernzweig, J., Karbon, M., Poulin, R., & Hanish, L. (1993). The relations of emotionality and regulation to preschoolers' social skills and sociometric status. *Child Development, 64*(5), 1418–1438.

Eisenberg, N., Fabes, R. A., & Murphy, B. C. (1996). Parents' reactions to children's negative emotions: Relations to children's social competence and comforting behavior. *Child Development, 67*(5), 2227–2247.

Eisenberg, N., Losoya, S., Fabes, R. A., Guthrie, I. K., Reiser, M., Murphy, B., Shepard, S. A., Poulin, R., & Padgett, S. J. (2001). Parental socialization of children's dysregulated expression of emotion and externalizing problems. *Journal of Family Psychology, 15*(2), 183–205.

Fabes, R. A., Poulin, R. E., Eisenberg, N., & Madden-Derdich, D. A. (2002). The coping with children's negative emotions scale (CCNES): Psychometric properties and relations with children's emotional competence. *Marriage & Family Review, 34*(3/4), 285–310.

Fantuzzo, J. W., Bulotsky-Shearer, R., Fusco, R. A., & McWayne, C. (2005). An investigation of preschool classroom behavioral adjustment problems and social-emotional school readiness competencies. *Early Childhood Research Quarterly, 20*(3), 259–275.

Fivush, R. (1991). Gender and emotion in mother-child conversations about the past. *Journal of Narrative & Life History, 1*(4), 325–341.

Fivush, R., Berlin, L. J., Sales, J. M., Mennuti-Washburn, J., & Cassidy, J. (2003). Functions of parent-child reminiscing about emotionally negative events. *Memory, 11*(2), 179–192.

Fivush, R., Brotman, M. A., Buckner, J. P., & Goodman, S. H. (2000). Gender differences in parent-child emotion narratives. *Sex Roles, 42*(3), 233–253.

Flannagan, D., & Perese, S. (1998). Emotional references in mother-daughter and mother-son dyads' conversations about school. *Sex Roles, 39*(5), 353–367.

Fredrickson, B. L. (1998). Cultivated emotions: Parental socialization of positive emotions and self-conscious emotions. *Psychological Inquiry, 9*(4), 279–281.

Garner, P. W., Jones, D. C., & Miner, J. L. (1994). Social competence among low-income preschoolers: Emotion socialization practices and social cognitive correlates. *Child Development, 65*(2), 622–637.

Garner, P. W., Robertson, S., & Smith, G. (1997). Preschool children's emotional expressions with peers: The roles of gender and emotion socialization. *Sex Roles*, 36(11/12), 675–691.

Garside, R. B., & Klimes-Dougan, B. (2002). Socialization of discrete negative emotions: Gender differences and links with psychological distress. *Sex Roles*, 47(3/4), 115–128.

Gross, D., & Harris, P. (1988). False beliefs about emotion: Children's understanding of misleading emotional displays. *International Journal of Behavioral Development*, 11(4), 475–488.

Halberstadt, A. G., et al. (1995). Self-expressiveness within the family context. *Psychological Assessment*, 7(1), 93–103.

Holmbeck, G. N. (2002). Post-hoc probing of significant moderational and mediational effects in studies of pediatric populations. *Journal of Pediatric Psychology*, 27(1), 87–96.

Hyson, M. C., & Lee, K. M. (1996). Assessing early childhood teachers' beliefs about emotions: Content, contexts, and implications for practice. *Early Education & Development*, 7(1), 59–78.

Klimes-Dougan, B., Brand, A. E., Zahn-Waxler, C., Usher, B., Hastings, P. D., Kendziora, K., & Garside, R. B. (2007). Parental emotion socialization in adolescence: Differences in sex, age and problem status. *Social Development*, 16(2), 326–342.

Kuebli, J., Butler, S., & Fivush, R. (1995). Mother-child talk about past emotions: Relations of maternal language and child gender over time. *Cognition & Emotion*, 9(2), 265–283.

Kuebli, J., & Fivush, R. (1992). Gender differences in parent-child conversations about past emotions. *Sex Roles*, 27(11–12), 683–698.

Lewis, C., & Lamb, M. E. (2003). Fathers' influences on children's development: The evidence from two-parent families. *European Journal of Psychology of Education*, 18(2), 211–228.

McElwain, N. L., Halberstadt, A. G., & Volling, B. L. (2007). Mother- and father-reported reactions to children's negative emotions: Relations to young children's emotional understanding and friendship quality. *Child Development*, 78(5), 1407–1425.

Miller, A. L., Fine, S. E., Gouley, K. K., Seifer, R., Dickstein, S., & Shields, A. (2006). Showing and telling about emotions: Interrelations between facets of emotional competence and associations with classroom adjustment in Head Start preschoolers. *Cognition & Emotion*, 20(8), 1170–1192.

Mirabile, S. P., Scaramella, L. V., Sohr-Preston, S. L., & Robison, S. D. (2009). Mothers' socialization of emotion regulation: The moderating role of children's negative emotional reactivity. *Child & Youth Care Forum*, 38(1), 19–37.

Racine, T. P., Carpendale, J. I. M., & Turnbull, W. (2007). Parent-child talk and children's understanding of beliefs and emotions. *Cognition & Emotion*, 21(3), 480–494.

Rothbart, M. K., Posner, M. I., & Kieras, J. (2006). Temperament, attention, and the development of self-regulation. In K. McCartney & D. Phillips (Eds.), *Blackwell handbook of early childhood development*. Malden, MA: Blackwell Publishing.

Shipman, K. L., Schneider, R., Fitzgerald, M. M., Sims, C., Swisher, L., & Edwards, A. (2007). Maternal emotion socialization in maltreating and non-maltreating families: Implications for children's emotion regulation. *Social Development*, 16(2), 268–285.

Thompson, R. A. (1991). Emotional regulation and emotional development. *Educational Psychology Review*, 3(4), 269–307.

Trentacosta, C. J., Izard, C. E., Mostow, A. J., & Fine, S. E. (2006). Children's emotional competence and attentional competence in early elementary school. *School Psychology Quarterly*, 21(2), 148–170.

Wong, M. S., McElwain, N. L., & Halberstadt, A. G. (2009). Parent, family, and child characteristics: Associations with mother- and father-reported emotion socialization practices. *Journal of Family Psychology, 23*(4), 452–463.
Zahn-Waxler, C., Shirtcliff, E., & Marceau, K. (2008). Disorders of childhood and adolescence: Gender and psychopathology. *Annual Review of Clinical Psychology, 4,* 275–303.

SUSANNE A. DENHAM is an applied developmental psychologist and professor of psychology at George Mason University. Her research focuses on children's social and emotional development. She is especially interested in the role of emotional competence in children's social and academic functioning. She is also investigating the development of forgiveness in children.

HIDEKO HAMADA BASSETT is currently working as a postdoctoral fellow with Susanne A. Denham on research of preschoolers' social and emotional aspects of school readiness at George Mason University in Fairfax, Virginia.

TODD M. WYATT is currently a doctoral candidate in applied developmental psychology at George Mason University in Fairfax, Virginia, and also holds the director of research position at Outside The Classroom, Inc., a public-health research and intervention firm based out of Boston.

Gender and Parents' Reactions to Children's Emotion During the Preschool Years

Amy Kennedy Root, Kenneth H. Rubin

Abstract

In this chapter, the authors examine the differences between mothers and fathers in the socialization of specific emotions in preschool-aged boys and girls. They argue that mothers and fathers play both distinct and complementary roles in the development of children's emotional competence; these roles are influenced both by parents' own gender, as well as the child's gender and the type of emotion being socialized. Through analyses of descriptive data, it appears that mothers and fathers respond to their children's emotions differently. The authors provide a discussion of the potential underlying reasons and potential implications for distinct emotion socialization by mothers and fathers. © Wiley Periodicals, Inc.

NEW DIRECTIONS FOR CHILD AND ADOLESCENT DEVELOPMENT, no. 128, Summer 2010 © Wiley Periodicals, Inc.
Published online in Wiley InterScience (www.interscience.wiley.com) • DOI: 10.1002/cd.268

Children who are emotionally competent are better prepared for school entry (Denham, 2006), are liked better by their peers (Shields & Cicchetti, 2001), and are more prosocial and socially competent (Eisenberg et al., 2001) than their emotionally incompetent counterparts. Children's emotional competence is thought to develop from a variety of factors, including how parents react to their emotional displays. Although parents' reactions to children's emotions are known to influence children's emotional competence, it is still unclear why some parents react to children's emotions in one way, whereas other parents react to the same emotion in a different manner. Both gender of parent and gender of child have been shown to impact the process of emotion socialization (see Chapter One), and it seems likely that parents will further alter their reactions to children's emotions depending on the type of emotion they are socializing. In this chapter, we attempt to answer some of the questions regarding why parents differ in their socialization practices by examining the ways that parent gender, child gender, and type of emotion (for example, happiness and anger) affect parents' responses to children's emotions. By understanding the factors that influence parents' socialization strategies, we will be able to provide caretakers, policy makers, and clinicians with a description of the factors that may help or hinder children's emotional development.

Review of the Relevant Literature

Given the central role that emotions play in children's development, it is not surprising that researchers have become increasingly interested in better understanding how children develop emotional competence (see Chapter One). In the early years of life, children learn the rules of emotional expression and gain the tools necessary for appropriate and effective expression and regulation of emotion through daily interactions with their parents. The process of learning about emotions—or emotion socialization—proceeds in direct and indirect ways (see Chapter One). One common way that socialization occurs is by parents' reactions to children's emotions; these interactions between parents and children likely occur several times per day. Thus, the study of parents' reactions to children's emotions provides an accurate view of how emotion socialization takes place in the "real world."

Indeed, parental reactions to children's emotions have been widely studied. The literature suggests that parents typically reinforce and encourage positive displays of affect while regulating and discouraging negative displays of emotion in their children. In general, parents who react to their children's emotions in a supportive and comforting way have children who are characterized as emotionally competent (Denham, 1997). On the other hand, parents who respond to their children's affect in an unsupportive fashion (for example, punitively) are thought to

New Directions for Child and Adolescent Development • DOI: 10.1002/cd

undermine their children's emotional development. For instance, mothers who endorse nonsupportive emotion socialization strategies (for example, minimizing children's emotion) have children that are emotionally dys-regulated and inexpressive in the classroom; moreover, these children are observed to flee or escape when encountering angry conflict situations in the peer group (an ineffective coping response) (Eisenberg & Fabes, 1994). In addition, parents who negatively reinforce (for example, verbal discouragement of emotional displays, punishment) their preschoolers' emotions at home have children who display less emotion knowledge when they are interviewed (Denham, Mitchell-Copeland, Strandberg, Auerbach, & Blair, 1997). Thus, it seems clear that parents who discredit or punish their children's emotions inhibit their children's abilities to express emotions, regulate emotions, and understand discrete emotional states. On the other hand, parents who are warm and supportive in response to their children's emotions have children who are emotionally competent (for example, Denham & Auerbach, 1995). However, the association between parents' socialization practices and children's emotional development is not without moderating factors, including gender.

Gender differences in the socialization of emotion are linked to the norms within the larger culture regarding the masculinity or femininity of specific emotions (Brody, 2000; Underwood, Coie, & Herbsman, 1992). As outlined in Chapter One, in North American cultures, there is evidence that the expression of internalizing affect is perceived to be nonmasculine, whereas emotions of an externalizing nature are viewed as nonfeminine. Indeed, empirical evidence supports the notion that the rules for the expression of emotions are different for boys and girls, and it appears that children understand these rules early in life (for example, Birnbaum, Nosanchuk, & Croll, 1980; Zeman & Shipman, 1996).

The differing rules for males and females may be rooted in temperamental differences between infant boys and girls in emotional expressiveness, with boys displaying less-positive affect and demonstrating greater difficulty in regulating negative arousal (Weinberg, Tronick, Cohn, & Olson, 1999); these differences may "set the stage" for different trajectories in emotional development. However, parents appear to play an important role in continuity and discontinuity of dispositional traits, including emotionality (for example, Crockenberg, 1987).

Indeed, gender differences in emotion socialization have been shown to emerge in infancy. For instance, mothers tend to match male infant emotional expressions more than female infant emotional expressions; further, mothers' imitation of joy increases over time when interacting with male infants, but decreases when interacting with female infants (Malatesta & Haviland, 1982). It is thought that mothers respond more contingently to their sons' positive affect than to their daughters' because of gender differences in irritability during the infancy period, with males reported as displaying more irritable and negative affect than females. Thus, mothers may feel a greater need to reinforce their sons' positive affect (via imitating emotional expressions) because of dispositional gender differences in affective displays (Malatesta & Haviland, 1982).

There has also been some evidence to suggest that the emotional interactions between mothers and their infants differ from those of fathers and their infants. For instance, infant arousal during mother–infant interaction appears to be manifested in an organized cycle of "low and medium states of arousal, with or without a single positive peak" (Feldman, 2003, p. 16). However, during father–infant interaction, positive arousal appears to be sudden (rather than gradual), and these episodes of peak positive emotion become more frequent during play (Feldman, 2003). Thus, it appears that mothers and fathers contribute to the development of "different modes of affective sharing and co-regulation" (Feldman, 2003, p. 17).

During the preschool years, gender differences in socialization continue. For instance, when parents and children are asked to discuss past emotional experiences, mothers and fathers differ in the use of emotion language with boys and girls (Adams, Kuebli, Boyle, & Fivush, 1995). Specifically, parents refer to emotions in their conversations with their preschool-aged daughters more often than in their discussions with their preschool-aged sons. Further, both fathers and mothers have been observed to discuss sadness and dislike more often with their daughters than their sons (Adams et al., 1995; Fivush Brotman, Buckner, & Goodman, 2000). Mothers and fathers also appear to differ in the *quality* of their emotional discussions depending on their child's gender; specifically, mothers and fathers appear to discuss emotions in the context of interpersonal relationships with their daughters more often than with their sons (Fivush et al., 2000). Further, as reviewed in Chapter One, there also appear to be differences between mothers' and fathers' reactions to sons' versus daughters' emotions, with anxiety or fear being more acceptable for girls and anger being more acceptable for boys (for example, Garner, Robertson, & Smith, 1997).

Thus, it is clear that gender does influence how parents respond to children's emotions; it is less clear, however, how parents respond to boys' and girls' *specific emotions*. By moving beyond responses to global emotions and illuminating the differences (and similarities) that exist between mothers' and fathers' reactions to specific emotions, it may be possible to better understand the concomitants of gender-differentiated emotion socialization. Hence, we examined the socialization of specific emotions, with the goal to better understand why and how parents react differently to boys' and girls' emotions.

Parent Gender, Child Gender, and Discrete Emotions as Factors in Emotion Socialization: A Descriptive Study

In this section, we present an empirically based description of how mothers and fathers differ in their responses to their sons' and daughters' displays of such varied emotions as happiness, disappointment, anger, and anxiety.

Participants. The participants comprised 125 parents (31 mothers of sons, 33 mothers of daughters, 28 fathers of sons, and 33 fathers of daughters) of preschool-aged children (child age $M = 3.87$; $SD = .79$; range 3 to 5 years). Participants were parents from the same household and reported only about biological children. The sample was restricted to two-parent, heterosexual families; no siblings were included in this study. Participants were largely drawn from preschools in and around the greater metropolitan Washington, D.C. area.

Demographic Questionnaire. Mothers and fathers completed a demographics questionnaire that consisted of five sections pertaining to parent age, ethnicity, education level, occupation, other persons living within the home, and approximate number of hours spent with his or her child on a daily basis.

The Emotion Stories Questionnaire. Mothers and fathers also completed a questionnaire based on a series of vignettes developed originally by Mills and Rubin (1990) in their research on parents' socialization beliefs and behaviors. The eight vignettes used herein have been used in past research (for example, Henderson, 1996). Each story depicted a child experiencing one of four emotions (happiness, anxiety, anger, or disappointment). Mothers and fathers were asked to imagine that the character in the story was his or her child. After reading each story, parents were asked to answer two questions: (1) "How would you *feel* when you see your child act in this manner?" Parents were asked to rate the following emotions on a five-point scale (1 = *Not at All* to 5 = *Extremely*): anger, disgust, embarrassment, anxiety, happiness, and sadness; and (2) "What, if anything, would you *do* in response to your child displaying happiness/anxiety/anger/disappointment just in front of you/in front of others?" Mothers' and fathers' responses were coded using a scheme originally developed by Mills and Rubin (1990; also see Henderson, 1996).

Responses were classified into a total of 21 specific categories. Within each story, each category was coded as either present in (1) or absent from (0) the rater's (either mother or father) report of his or her behavior. Relevant categories for this investigation were limited to those parental responses regarding children's emotions. Specifically, we were interested in examining the following emotion socialization strategies: direct/indirect command-feelings (for example, "Stop crying"), question feelings (for

NEW DIRECTIONS FOR CHILD and ADOLESCENT DEVELOPMENT • DOI: 10.1002/cd

example, "Tell me how your feeling"), and support-acknowledge feelings (for example, "Tell her it is okay to feel anxious").

We were also interested in investigating parents' negative reactions to children's emotions; therefore, we examined the following emotion socialization strategies: punishment (for example, "Send him to time out") and criticize child/behavior (for example, "That's not a nice way to act when someone gives you a gift"). We chose to examine the specific emotion socialization strategies listed above (rather than examining global socialization strategies such as supportive reactions) to identify parents' precise responses to their sons' and daughters' different emotion displays.

A parent could respond with a single strategy (for example, "I would pick him up and leave the store") or multiple strategies (for example, "I would ask him what happened and then give him a hug"); for the same story; therefore, the codes were summed within emotion, and proportionalized.

Reliability. Mothers' and fathers' responses to the questions "What, if anything, might you do in response to your child displaying (happiness/ anxiety/anger/ disappointment) in (front of others/just in front of you) were coded by two coders. Reliability was calculated on 20% of the sample and Cohen's kappa was .83 over all codes.

Results

We compared four groups (mothers of sons, mothers of daughters, fathers of sons, and fathers of daughters) on parents' reports of emotional reactions and socialization strategies. A series of analyses of variance (ANOVA) was conducted to examine if differences existed between the four groups.

In the first set of ANOVAs, we compared the groups on their emotional reactions and socialization strategies to the happiness stories. As depicted in Figure 4.1, mothers reported significantly more happiness in response to a story of their daughters' happiness than fathers of daughters or fathers of sons.

Next, we examined the differences between the groups in the emotional reactions and socialization strategies offered in response to the anxiety stories. Fathers reported significantly more surprise to a story of their son's display of anxiety than mothers of daughters and fathers of daughters (see Figure 4.2). There were also differences between the four groups in the emotion socialization strategies offered in response to children's displays of anxiety. Fathers reported they would respond to their son's anxiety depicted in a vignette with answers categorized as support/ acknowledge feelings (for example, "I would reassure him that it is okay be scared") significantly more than mothers of sons (see Figure 4.3). Further, mothers reported they would respond to a story of their daughters' displays of anxiety with answers categorized as question feelings (for

NEW DIRECTIONS FOR CHILD and ADOLESCENT DEVELOPMENT • DOI: 10.1002/cd

Figure 4.1. Mothers' and Fathers' Report of Happiness to Happy Stories

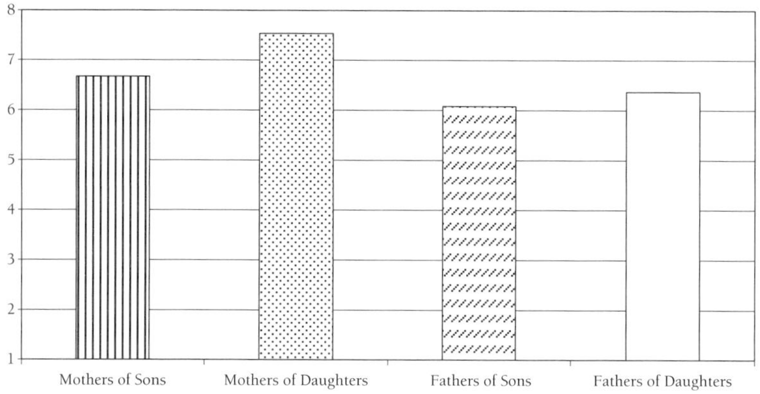

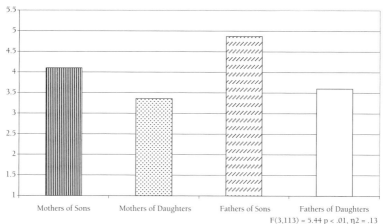

F(3,113) = 3.71, p < .05, η2 = .09

Figure 4.2. Mothers' and Fathers' Report of Surprise to Anxiety Stories

F(3,113) = 5.44 p < .01, η2 = .13

example, "I would ask her why she's uncomfortable") significantly more often than fathers of sons and fathers of daughters (see Figure 4.4). Thus, it appears that both mothers and fathers respond to their same-gendered child's emotions in a supportive fashion, although they utilize different types of strategies.

We next analyzed the data regarding children's displays of anger. There were no significant differences between the groups in the reactions or socialization strategies offered to the anger stories.

Figure 4.3. Mothers' and Fathers' Report of Support/Acknowledge Feelings to the Anxiety Stories

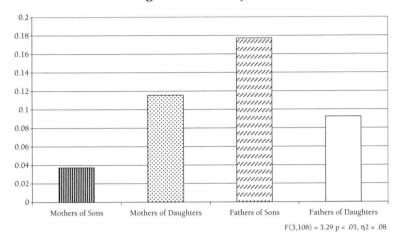

F(3,108) = 3.29 p < .05, η2 = .08

Figure 4.4. Mothers' and Fathers' Report of Question Feelings to Anxiety Stories

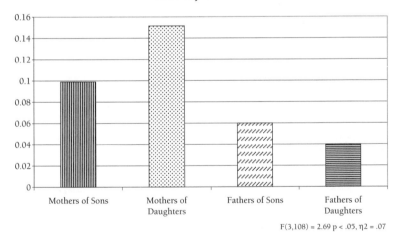

F(3,108) = 2.69 p < .05, η2 = .07

Finally, we examined the differences between the four groups in the emotional reactions and socialization strategies offered in response to children's display of disappointment. As shown in Figure 4.5, mothers of daughters reported significantly more disgust to their daughters' displays of disappointment depicted in a hypothetical story than mothers of sons and fathers of daughters. Furthermore, fathers reported more disgust to

Figure 4.5. Mothers' and Fathers' Report of Disgust to Disappointment Stories

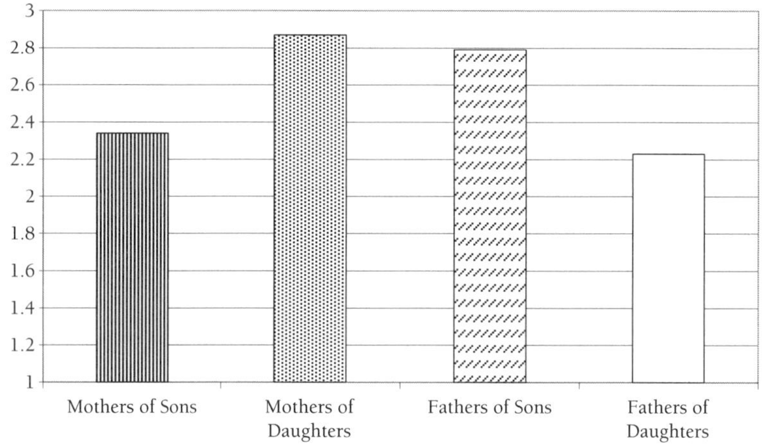

$$F(3,112) = 4.43 \; p < .001, \; \eta2 = .11$$

their son's displays of disappointment than mothers of sons and fathers of daughters. Thus, it appears that parents report greater disgust to their same-gendered child's display of disappointment.

Discussion and Conclusions

The goal of this chapter was to examine the gender differences that emerge in the socialization of specific emotions, with a focus on the differences (and similarities) between mothers and fathers. It seems important to better understand how gender influences mothers' and fathers' responses to children's emotion as different responses may impact children's later socioemotional development, especially for those children considered at risk. We found evidence that mothers and fathers differentiate their emotional reactions to their sons' and daughters' displays of the same emotion. For instance, mothers reported responding with more happiness to their daughters' happiness in a hypothetical story than did fathers of sons and fathers of daughters. Taken alone, one might conclude that males may not be as expressive as females; thus fathers may not have reported strong emotional reactions in response to the happiness vignettes. Previous research supports this notion (for example, Brody & Hall, 1993; Jansz, 2000). However, others have reported that males and females do not differ in the expression of *positive* emotions (Fischer, 1993). An alternate explanation may be that parents take on distinct parenting roles and

NEW DIRECTIONS FOR CHILD and ADOLESCENT DEVELOPMENT • DOI: 10.1002/cd

responsibilities. It may be that mothers view that a central role they play in their daughters' lives is to reinforce the expression of positive emotions, whereas fathers may not view the socialization of positive affect as a high priority, especially for their sons.

Further support for the notion that parents may respond differently to their sons' and daughters' emotions was found herein. Specifically, mothers and fathers differed in their responses to their children's anxiety, depending on their child's gender; fathers reported that they would respond with significantly more surprise to their sons' displays of anxiety than fathers of daughters and mothers of daughters. This is not surprising, given that anxiety has been characterized as a nonmasculine emotion (Jansz, 2000). Therefore, it may be that fathers do not expect their sons to display anxious behavior because boys' displays of internalizing emotions are discouraged and punished in Western culture (Jansz, 2000). Indeed, fathers do report less engagement with their fearful sons (MacDonald & Parke, 1984), and males also receive negative reinforcement for the display of internalizing affect outside of the home (Coplan, Gavinski-Molina, Lagace-Seguin, & Wichmann, 2001; Stevenson-Hinde & Glover, 1996).

Although parents' different emotional responses provide evidence for the distinct emotional climates provided for boys and girls, parents' emotional reactions to children's emotions only tell part of the story. It seems that understanding how parents deal with their children's emotions (in other words, the strategies they report) will provide insight to understanding how children learn the rules for emotional expression. In this investigation we found some evidence to suggest that mothers and fathers also alter the strategies they use in response to their children's emotion by child gender. Specifically, fathers reported they would reassure (support/ acknowledge feelings) their sons' feelings of anxiety (as depicted in a story) more often than mothers of sons. Thus, it appears that fathers, although surprised about their sons' display of anxiety, report that they would attempt to soothe their sons' fears. Interestingly, when mothers were asked to report their responses to their children's anxiety, mothers of daughters reported they would ask for more information (question feelings) when their daughters were expressing anxiety more often than fathers of daughters. Taken together, it seems that both mothers and fathers respond to their same-gendered children's expressions of anxiety in a different manner, yet both appear to be sensitive and supportive. To fully understand the differences (or similarities) between mothers' and fathers' reactions to their children's anxiety it would be important to understand what transpires after the initial response. Does further conversation or explanation of emotion occur between parent and child? This is a crucial question for future researchers to address given that research indicates that the *quality* of parent–child discussion is extremely important in children's emotional development (for example, Denham & Auerbach, 1995)

It is important to note that the findings regarding fathers' supportive responses to their sons' anxiety are contrary to the existing literature regarding gender-stereotyped emotion socialization (for example, fathers discuss sadness more often with daughters than sons) (Adams et al., 1995); it may be that there has been a generational shift since the early 1990s in fathers' investment in their sons' emotional lives. This may be a result of recent media attention given to the pitfalls of the Western ideal of the "emotionally inexpressive male." For instance, the National Institute of Mental Health launched a media campaign to bring attention to the growing number of men silently suffering from internalizing disorders in the mid-2000's (for example, Kersting, 2005). Furthermore, several popular psychology books have brought attention to addressing the problems associated with the proliferation of masculine stereotypes in Western culture (for example, Kindlon & Thomson, 1999). Thus, it may be that fathers are paying particular attention to their sons' emotion displays, and responding with sensitivity. Furthermore, it is also likely that these views are a reflection of a modern, dual-income family where parenting roles are more likely to be evenly distributed across caregivers. Indeed, it has been noted that families who endorse more egalitarian or feminist views of child-rearing are less likely to display gender-typed behavior (for example, Kulik, 2002).

The *differences* between mothers' and fathers' reactions to children's emotion are a small piece of the complex process of emotion socialization. Given that parents and children comprise the larger family system, it is likely that both mothers and fathers also carry similar philosophies about effective child-rearing. Certainly, one would expect for mothers' and fathers' parenting beliefs to converge on many areas, especially where they need to teach their children essential life skills. Indeed, we found some similarities in the responses mothers and fathers reported. For instance, mothers of daughters and fathers of sons reported significantly more disgust in response to their children's displays of disappointment than mothers of sons and fathers of daughters. We feel that this finding may be a reflection of parents' effort to socialize good behavior (one of the disappointment stories was about the child receiving a gift they did not like); if this is indeed the case, one may wonder, "Why did they not react in the same manner toward their opposite sex child?" It may be that it is the same-gendered parents' role to socialize good behavior. Indeed, it has been suggested that the same-gendered parent may be the best socializer for the development of altruistic behavior (Eisenberg, Fabes, Carlo, & Karbon, 1992; Hastings, Rubin, & DeRose, 2005).

Taken together, it appears that there are similarities and differences in the way that mothers and fathers respond to their children's emotions, which are influenced by both child gender and emotion type. Specifically, it appears that mothers and fathers are particularly invested in teaching their same-gendered child about appropriate expression and regulation of emotions. Importantly, it seems that—in this sample—both mothers and fathers respond in supportive ways to their children's emotions (as evidenced in the responses to the anxiety stories); however, they do so in unique ways, which is perhaps a reflection of their gender. Moreover, although these differences exist between mothers' and fathers' emotion socialization, there appear to be similar goals between mothers and fathers in how they'd like their children to behave (as evidenced in the disappointment stories). Therefore, we've provided evidence that underscores the importance of both mothers and fathers in socialization of emotion.

Although we examined processes of emotion socialization that are relatively understudied, there were limitations to this study. To begin, it is important to note that, although there was diversity in the sample in terms of race/ethnicity, the sample was homogeneous in socioeconomic status (SES), with the majority of the sample representing middle to upper-middle class. There are few studies investigating emotion socialization practices in low-SES samples (for an exception see Chapter Two), and far fewer with fathers from low-SES samples. Indeed, it is documented that mothers in a low-SES group respond differently to their children's emotions than mothers in a middle-SES group (Martini, Root, & Jenkins, 2004). Thus, it is important to keep in mind that the results presented herein are not universal. Further, it is important to note that the use of single informants herein does not allow for generalizability beyond parents' beliefs about their emotion socialization strategies.

In sum, by examining the socialization of specific emotions by mothers and fathers we have provided a framework to better understand how gender and emotion type impact the emotion socialization process. The findings support the notion that mothers and fathers are both invested in their children's emotional lives, but that their roles differ depending on child gender and type of emotion their child is displaying.

Although, the impact of gender-specific and emotion-specific socialization on children's emotional development was not examined in the present study, it is likely that the manner which mothers and fathers react to their sons' versus daughters' specific emotions affects the development of children's emotional competence. Moreover, it has been suggested that reinforcing some emotions and discouraging others may place some children at risk for the development of psychopathology (see Chapter Two for relevant discussion); therefore, by better understanding the normative differences (and similarities) that emerge in mothers' and fathers' reactions to children's emotions, it is possible to better understand how mothers and fathers can foster the development of emotional competence. Indeed, the findings support the notion that mothers and fathers play different, yet also overlapping, roles in the socialization of their children's emotions. Further examination of these roles may provide a better understanding of how to best promote successful emotional development in young children.

References

Adams, S., Kuebli, J., Boyle, P. A., & Fivush, R. (1995). Gender differences in parent-child conversations about past emotions: A longitudinal investigation. *Sex Roles, 33,* 309–323.

Birnbaum, D. W., Nosanchuk, T. A., & Croll, W. L. (1980). Children's stereotypes about sex differences in emotionality. *Sex Roles, 6,* 435–443.

Brody, L. R. (2000). The socialization of gender differences in emotional expression: Display rules, infant temperament, and differentiation. In A. H. Fischer (Ed.), *Gender and emotion: Social psychological perspectives* (pp. 24–47). Cambridge, UK: Cambridge University Press.

Brody, L. R., & Hall, J. A. (1993). Gender and emotion. In M. Lewis & J. Haviland (Eds.), *Handbook of emotions* (pp. 447–460). New York: Guilford.

Coplan, R. J., Gavinski-Molina, M., Lagace-Seguin, D., & Wichmann, C. (2001). When girls versus boys play alone: Nonsocial play and adjustment in kindergarten. *Developmental Psychology, 37,* 464–474.

Crockenberg, S. (1987). Predictors and correlates of anger toward and punitive control of toddlers by adolescent mothers. *Child Development, 58,* 964–975.

Denham, S. A. (1997). When I have a bad dream, mommy holds me: Preschoolers' conceptions of emotions, parental socialization, and emotional competence. *International Journal of Behavioral Development, 20,* 301–319.

Denham, S. A. (2006). Social-emotional competence as support for school readiness: What is it and how do we assess it? *Early Education and Development, 17,* 57–89.

Denham, S. A., & Auerbach, S. (1995). Mother-child dialogue about emotions and preschoolers' emotion comptence. *Social and General Psychology Monographs, 121,* 313–338.

Denham, S. A., Mitchell-Copeland, J., Strandberg, K., Auerbach, S., & Blair, K. (1997). Parental contributions to preschoolers' emotional competence: Direct and indirect effects. *Motivation & Emotion, 21,* 65–86.

Eisenberg, N., & Fabes, R. A. (1994). Mothers' reactions to children's negative emotions: Relations to children's temperament and anger behavior. *Merrill-Palmer Quarterly, 40,* 138–156.

Eisenberg, N., Fabes, R. A., Carlo, G., & Karbon, M. (1992). Emotional responsivity to others: Behavioral correlates and socialization antecedents. *New Directions in Child Development, 55,* 57–73.

Eisenberg, N., Losoya, S., Fabes, R. A., Guthrie, I. K., Reiser, M., Murphy, B., Shepard, S. A., Poulin, R., & Padgett, S. J. (2001). Parental socialization of children's dysregulated expression of emotion and externalizing problems. *Journal of Family Psychology, 15,* 183–205.

Feldman, R. (2003). Infant-mother and infant-father synchrony: The coregulation of positive arousal. *Infant Mental Health Journal, 24,* 1–23.

Fischer, A. H. (1993). Sex differences in emotionality. *Feminism and Psychology, 3,* 303–318.

Fivush, R., Brotman, M. A., Buckner, J. P., & Goodman, S. H. (2000). Gender differences in parent-child emotion narratives. *Sex Roles, 42,* 233–253.

Garner, P. W., Robertson, S., & Smith, G. (1997). Preschool children's emotional expressions with peers: The roles of gender and emotion socialization. *Sex Roles, 36,* 675–691.

Hastings, P. D., Rubin, K. H., & DeRose, L. (2005). Links among gender, inhibition, and parental socialization in the development of prosocial behavior. *Merrill-Palmer Quarterly, 51(4),* 467–493.

Henderson, H. A. (1996). The socialization of emotion regulation: A mediator of physiological predispositions towards social withdrawal? Unpublished Master's thesis: University of Guelph.

Jansz, J. (2000). Masculine identity and restrictive emotionality. In A. H. Fischer (Ed.), *Gender and emotion: Social psychological perspectives* (pp. 166–185). Cambridge, UK: Cambridge University Press.

Kersting, K. (2005). Men and depression: Battling stigma through public education. *APA Monitor on Psychology, 36*, 66.

Kindlon, D., & Thomson, M. (1999). *Raising Cain: Protecting the emotional life of boys.* Toronto: Ballantine.

Kulik, L. (2002). The impact of social background on gender-role ideology: Parents' versus children's attitudes. *Journal of Family Issues, 23*, 53–73.

MacDonald, K., & Parke, R. D. (1984). Bridging the gap: Parent-child play interaction and peer interactive competence. *Child Development, 55*, 1265–1277.

Malatesta, C. Z., & Haviland, J. M. (1982). Learning display rules: The socialization of emotion expression in infancy. *Child Development, 53*, 991–1003.

Martini, T. S., Root, C. A., & Jenkins, J. M. (2004). Low and middle income mothers' regulation of negative emotion: Effects of children's temperament and situational emotional responses. *Social Development, 13*, 515–530.

Mills, R. S. L., & Rubin, K. H. (1990). Parental beliefs about problematic social behaviors in early childhood. *Child Development, 61*, 138–151.

Shields, A., & Cicchetti, D. (2001). Parental maltreatment and emotion dysregulation as risk factors for bullying and victimization in middle childhood. *Journal of Clinical Child Psychology, 30*, 349–363.

Stevenson-Hinde, J., & Glover, A. (1996). Shy girls and boys: A new look. *Journal of Child Psychology and Psychiatry and Allied Disciplines, 37*, 181–187.

Underwood, M. K., Coie, J. D., & Herbsman, C. R. (1992). Display rules for anger and aggression in school-age children. *Child Development, 63*, 366–380.

Weinberg, M. K., Tronick, E. Z., Cohn, J. F., & Olson, K. L. (1999). Gender differences in emotional expressivity and self regulation during early infancy. *Developmental Psychology, 35*, 175–188.

Zeman, J., & Shipman, K. (1996). Children's expression of negative affect: Reasons and methods. *Developmental Psychology, 32*, 842–849.

AMY KENNEDY ROOT *is an assistant professor of child development and family studies at West Virginia University. Her research interests include understanding how children's dispositional characteristics and caregiving experiences work together (or against one another) to impact children's socioemotional development throughout the early childhood years.*

KENNETH H. RUBIN *is professor of human development and director of the Center for Children, Relationships, and Culture at the University of Maryland, College Park. His research interests include the study of peer and parent child interactions and relationships, social and emotional adjustment, culture and development, and the origins of social competence.*

Zeman, J., Perry-Parish, C., & Cassano, M. (2010). Parent-child discussions of anger and sadness: The importance of parent and child gender during middle childhood. In A. Kennedy Root & S. Denham (Eds.), *The role of gender in the socialization of emotion: Key concepts and critical issues. New Directions for Child and Adolescent Development, 128,* 65–83. San Francisco: Jossey-Bass.

5

Parent-Child Discussions of Anger and Sadness: The Importance of Parent and Child Gender During Middle Childhood

Janice Zeman, Carisa Perry-Parrish, Michael Cassano

Abstract

This chapter provides conceptual background and empirical evidence that parental emotion socialization continues well into middle childhood and is influenced by the social context. Data are presented to illustrate the influence of parent and child gender on parental socialization of emotion in 113 Caucasian, middle-class children. Mothers and fathers discussed historical sadness- and anger-eliciting events with their sons and daughters. Fathers appear to play a unique role in sadness socialization whereas mothers' influence seems distinctive for the socialization of anger. Socialization of emotion is a transactional process in which parents and children are both socializing agents and emotion regulators. © Wiley Periodicals, Inc.

NEW DIRECTIONS FOR CHILD AND ADOLESCENT DEVELOPMENT, no. 128, Summer 2010 © Wiley Periodicals, Inc.
Published online in Wiley InterScience (www.interscience.wiley.com) • DOI: 10.1002/cd.269

It has been written that "[s]ociety determines children's understanding of emotions by inducting them into an emotional culture, defining the criteria of emotional competence, and regulating their exposure to emotional episodes" (Gordon, 1989, p. 319). Parents are typically the most important influence on the development of emotion regulation (ER), particularly in early childhood. Operating as a bidirectional process, parental socialization contributes to and is directly influenced by children's developing ER abilities by structuring a child's emotional world and shaping emotional understanding and regulation strategies (Denham, 1998; Thompson, 1990). Furthermore, pathways of parental socialization vary as a function of parent gender, child gender, and emotion type (Thompson & Meyer, 2007). It is not clear, however, how far-reaching the effects of parental influence on emotion socialization become as children progress beyond the early childhood period.

Middle childhood (roughly ages 5 through 11) is a particularly important stage of development to consider for emotion socialization because of the accompanying biological, social, and cognitive changes that influence affective and regulatory processes. For example, across middle childhood, children gradually gain self-regulation abilities associated with neurological growth in centers of the brain responsible for executive functioning. With the realm of cognitive development, children's increasing skills in perspective taking, recursive thinking, memory, language, and problem solving certainly impact their abilities to manage emotions within social contexts. Regarding social development, forming social ties with peers and increased involvement in structured and nonstructured peer interactions provide numerous opportunities to practice skills related to emerging emotional competencies. Further, research has indicated that the family environment provides the scaffolding and foundation for social–emotional skills that are enacted within other social contexts (Sroufe, 2005). Thus, it is surprising that this important stage of development is only now beginning to receive some attention within the emotion development domain (Klimes-Dougan & Zeman, 2007).

In this chapter, our overarching goal is to present theory and research on how parent and child gender shape ER processes in middle childhood and how these may differ depending on the type of emotion discussed. We will first present a very brief overview of gender socialization followed by a discussion of emotion socialization processes with an emphasis on the role of child and parent gender differences in emotion discussions. To complement the theoretical review, we present data that uses a parent-child discussion task in which we focus explicitly on same- and cross-sex parent-child dyads to investigate the contributions of both parent and child gender to emotion socialization in middle childhood. We conclude with a discussion that highlights the implications of gender in parental emotion socialization.

NEW DIRECTIONS FOR CHILD and ADOLESCENT DEVELOPMENT • DOI: 10.1002/cd

Gender Socialization by Parents

Gender differences in children's behavior are often attributed to parental socialization; however, the most surprising outcome of studies that focus on gender-related socialization practices is an abundance of null findings and small effect sizes. A meta-analysis of parental socialization practices indicated that parents', particularly fathers', encouragement of sex-typed activities was the most stable significant finding (Lytton & Romney, 1991). Fathers are more active than mothers in gender socialization of children, but only with sons (Maccoby, 1998). Fathers are also more likely to differentiate between sons and daughters than are mothers and tend to be stricter and more negative with sons (Siegal, 1987). Although the detection of gender differences in children's social behavior appears related to the method of assessment (Maccoby, 1990), measurement of emotional expressivity, however, reveals gender differences regardless of the methodology, either when children are tested individually with an experimenter (McDowell, O'Neil, & Parke, 2000; Saarni, 1984) or responding to self-report questionnaires (Zeman & Garber, 1996; Zeman & Shipman, 1996). Emotion theorists assert that gender is a crucial component within the social context that shapes children's emotional expressivity and regulation (Halberstadt, Denham, & Dunsmore, 2001).

Types of Emotion Socialization Processes. Parent-child interactions are considered the primary forum for emotion socialization during the childhood years and provide the basis for children's developing ER abilities. Parents influence children's ER through a variety of developmental pathways, including indirect and direct methods (see Chapter One in this volume for more detail). Our focus in this chapter is on direct socialization methods in middle childhood; this emphasis is intended to complement and extend the historical focus on maternal interactions with preschool children. Accordingly, we provide a brief overview of one type of direct socialization method, followed by a more in-depth synopsis of research on parent-child emotion discussions, the primary methodological focus of this chapter.

Parental Emotion Philosophy. According to Eisenberg, Spinrad, and Cumberland (1998), "parental socialization of emotion involves parenting behaviors that reflect parental beliefs, goals, and values in regard to their children's experience, expression, and modulation of emotion" (p. 317). Parents' emotion philosophy also encompasses meta-emotion theory (Gottman, Katz, & Hooven, 1996), which proposes that the quality of the parent-child emotional connection (for example, sensitivity, availability, parent-child emotion talk) and parental behavioral control (for example, modeling and reinforcing appropriate emotion display rules) influence the development of children's ER. Two parenting styles have been described. An *emotion coaching* parenting style views a child's experience of negative affect as generally healthy and an opportunity for teaching. These parents appear to be more "tuned-in" to their children's emotional experiences as well as their own, regulate their own emotional reactions to children's affective experiences, set clear behavioral limits for emotional behavior, communicate empathic concern and understanding, attempt to understand their child's feelings, help their child to verbally label feelings, and problem-solve with their child to find the most constructive way to manage emotional situations.

On the other hand, *emotion dismissing* parents view negative affect as harmful to the child and attempt to protect children from experiencing negative emotions. Accordingly, these parents lack a rich emotion vocabulary, fail to notice lower intensity emotions in children and themselves, become increasingly distressed by their children's negative emotions, discourage emotional introspection, and often fail to allow children to make attempts at self-regulation (Gottman et al., 1996). As research provides initial support for the role of meta-emotion philosophy in parental socialization of emotion (Gottman et al., 1996; Lunkenheimer, Shields, & Cortina, 2007), our goal was to examine how mothers and fathers may differentially respond to their sons' and daughters' discussions of sadness and anger with coaching and dismissing styles during the understudied developmental period of middle childhood. Parents' responses to these negative emotions in their children during middle childhood may promote or interfere with current and subsequent healthy emotional development, including the development of ER skills. Further, as most research has focused on mother-child discussions of emotion, another goal was to explore whether fathers play a different and/or complementary role in their emotion socialization efforts.

Influence of Parent and Child Gender on Emotion Discussions. Research has indicated that large differences exist between families and parents regarding the frequency and nature of conversations about emotion (Bretherton, Fritz, & Zahn-Waxler, 1986; Cervantes & Callanan, 1998). Further, emotion conversations appear to be directly linked to the development of facets of ER, including emotional understanding and expressivity. As discussed elsewhere (Chapter Three, this volume), research has revealed the salience of maternal conversations of emotion with young children. As children move beyond the preschool years, cognitive and affective maturation likely influences conversations about emotion; for example, age differences in emotion discussions may reflect changes in emotional understanding. However, more research that includes both parents is needed to examine this developmental trajectory into middle childhood.

Child Gender Differences in Emotion Conversation. Gender differences in parental socialization of ER through discussion with their young children are well established in the literature and primarily focus on preschool children (see Chapter One, this volume, Cervantes & Callanan, 1998;

Dunn, Bretherton, & Munn, 1987). Detailed analyses of parent-child conversations conducted by Fivush and colleagues (Adams, Kuebli, Boyle, & Fivush, 1995; Fivush, 1989; Fivush, Brotman, Buckner, & Goodman, 2000) have indicated several differences as a function of parent and child gender. For example, although mothers used approximately the same number of emotion words with their 3-year-old boys and girls, they used proportionately more positive than negative emotion words with girls only. In addition, when negative emotions were discussed with girls, mothers typically attributed the cause of the emotion to someone other than their daughter; this finding did not emerge for boys. Finally, mothers rarely discussed anger with girls, but did so frequently with boys. By comparison, mothers (Adams et al., 1995; Fivush, 1989) and fathers (Fivush et al., 2000) discussed sadness more frequently with daughters than with sons, even though girls did not initiate conversations about sadness more than boys (Fivush et al., 2000). Thus, it appears that mothers and fathers may engage in gender-specific socialization of their children's emotions even when behavioral differences are absent.

Parent Gender Differences in Emotion Conversation. Our primary goal was to investigate potential differences and similarities between mothers and fathers given the paucity of research involving fathers (Cassano, Adrian, Veits, & Zeman, 2006). The small base of studies using both mothers and fathers reveals interesting differences. For example, parents and their 4-year-old children were instructed to discuss times when the child experienced happiness, anger, sadness, and fear (Fivush et al., 2000). Conversations involving mothers were longer, involved more in-depth discussion of the emotional state, and contained more emotion words than those with fathers. Interestingly, mothers and fathers used significantly more emotion-related language and were more likely to discuss emotional experiences within an interpersonal context when discussing sadness with girls compared to boys (Fivush and others, 2000), which has also been observed in 3- to 6-year-old children (Adams et al., 1995).

Unique socialization pathways appear to exist in middle childhood. Age differences in children's ER strategies are demonstrated by increasing sophistication in abilities to modify expressions of emotions and manage emotional difficulties (Saarni, 1999), indicating a need for studies that identify potential influences on these developmental changes. Moreover, parents' expectations of their children's regulation abilities may change throughout development as well, either in response to maturation or in anticipation of such growth. Parental expectations may reflect specific gender socialization goals as well that then influence children's developing ER skills. Accordingly, a secondary aim was to improve our understanding of parent and child discussions of emotion during this understudied developmental period.

Parent and child gender differences emerged when 9- to 10-year-old children and their mothers and fathers were instructed to discuss situations that are difficult to manage (McDowell, Kim, O'Neil, & Parke, 2002). There was a positive association between boys' levels of sadness expression and fathers' tendency to blame their sons for the discussed situation. Boys who exhibited higher rates of dysregulated sadness and anger had mothers and fathers who tended to focus on the child's contribution to the difficult situation. Boys' anger dysregulation was also negatively related to maternal positive expressivity. Mothers who exhibited less-controlling and more-positive expressivity had girls who regulated emotion more effectively. In sum, this brief overview of the emotion socialization literature suggests that parental socialization may be differentially guided by parent gender, child gender, and the interactions between parent and child gender.

Despite the growing literature regarding emotional development, there are several significant gaps in our current understanding of the parental socialization of emotion. First, reflective of developmental and child clinical literature in general (Cassano et al., 2006), fathers have rarely been included in research examining socialization processes. As has been noted, fathers may respond in unique ways to their children's emotional expressivity that may vary as a function of emotion type and child gender. Second, methodologies tend to rely on maternal self-report of their hypothetical responses to their child's emotional behavior; few studies have directly observed parenting behaviors in an emotion-socialization context, particularly in middle childhood. To illustrate this point, we present data from a parent-child emotion discussion task. This methodology has not been widely used past the preschool years, yet children and their parents continue to discuss and confront emotional expressivity in daily life. Moreover, there may be changes in parent-child emotion discussions that reflect children's maturing ER abilities and emotional understanding, as well as changes in parental expectations of the same. Thus, emotion discussions have the potential to provide an ecologically valid way to gain important insights into the nature of socialization processes during the middle childhood years as well. Third, rather than assessing global negative emotionality, we chose to examine sadness and anger as separate constructs to determine whether there are different patterns of socialization by mothers and fathers for these emotions. Based on meta-emotion theory and functionalist approaches to emotion, we would expect that parents and children may hold different expectations regarding the acceptability of experiencing and expressing sadness versus anger. We anticipate that these expectations are also influenced by the developmental status and gender of the child. Taken together, our research adds to the literature by directly examining both mothers' and fathers' emotion socialization behaviors using a parent-child discussion task involving children in middle childhood.

NEW DIRECTIONS FOR CHILD and ADOLESCENT DEVELOPMENT • DOI: 10.1002/cd

A Study of Parental Discussions of Anger and Sadness with Their Sons and Daughters

For our study, 53 fathers and 60 mothers of 6- to 11-year-old daughters ($n = 59$) and sons ($n = 54$) were recruited from local public school systems in a small urban, northeastern region as part of a larger study examining parental socialization of emotion (Cassano, Zeman, & Perry-Parrish, 2007). Two child age groups were formed: younger ($n = 57$, first through second grades; M age = 7.16 years SD = .80) and older ($n = 56$, fourth through fifth grades; M age = 12.08 years, SD = .80). Regarding ethnicity, 95% of the participants were Caucasian and from middle-to upper-class socioeconomic status. Most children lived with their biological parents (80.4%), with the remainder living with their mother only (12.5%), mother and stepfather (6.3%), and father only (0.9%).

One biological parent and one child of the target age per family participated in an audiotaped discussion task in which the parent was told, "We would like you to talk with your child about a time when he or she felt sad and a time when he or she felt mad. There are no right or wrong answers, and the conversation can be as long or as short as you would like." Parent-child dyads were instructed to discuss the sadness- and anger-evoking events together, which typically took 5 to 10 minutes. The majority (95%) of discussion tasks took place in the participants' home with the remainder conducted in a university laboratory. The audiotapes were transcribed by a team of research assistants and coded by the third author (M.C.) into the following categories.

First, the *content* of the discussions was coded into representative categories by emotion type (see Table 5.1). The *length of conversation*

Table 5.1. Percent Endorsement (Number of Children) of Topics for Parent-Child Discussion Task

Sadness	Boys	Girls	Both
Loss of pet	35% (19)	45% (25)	44% (40)
Loss of family member/close relation	20% (11)	24% (13)	22% (24)
Loss of possession/privilege	20% (11)	13% (7)	16% (18)
Getting in trouble	19% (10)	5% (3)	12% (13)
Missing social event	4% (2)	11% (6)	7% (8)
Missing parents (e.g., when at school)	0	5% (3)	3% (3)
Other	2% (1)	4% (2)	3% (3)
Anger			
Conflict with peer (sibling, friend)	24% (13)	46% (26)	35% (39)
Loss of possession/privilege	39% (21)	27% (15)	32% (36)
Getting into trouble with parents or teachers	35% (19)	18% (10)	26% (29)
Other	2% (1)	9% (5)	5% (6)

NEW DIRECTIONS FOR CHILD and ADOLESCENT DEVELOPMENT • DOI: 10.1002/cd

provided an assessment of the opportunity for socialization around emotional experience to occur. This code consisted of the total number of words spoken by the child and the parent, but did not assess for the time the conversation took given that people have different rates of spoken language. The *proportion of words spoken by the parent* was a ratio of parent talk to child talk and provided an evaluation of who was leading the conversation. The *number of negative emotion words* related to anger or sadness (for example, upset, angry, disappointed) used by the parent provided an assessment of how parents modeled responding to negative emotional events for their child.

Finally, each proposition in the discussion was identified and defined as a subject-verb statement (for example, "I cried"). Then, consistent with Gottman et al.'s (1996) research, relevant propositions were classified as emotion-coaching (EC), or emotion-dismissing (ED) based on a coding system utilized by Lunkenheimer et al. (2007). Propositions coded as EC were defined as parents' verbal statements and questions regarding their child's emotions that validate the experience, label the affect, or assist in generating or evaluating behavioral responses to the emotional event (for example, "I could tell that you were sad because you didn't want to play outside"). ED propositions were defined as parents' verbal statements and questions that do not validate the child's experience, avoid discussing the event, criticize the child, minimize the child's experience, distract the child from the emotional event or the task itself, or communicate that it is inappropriate to be discussing feelings. Propositions were also coded as ED if the statement or question interrupts the child, ridicules the child, constitutes an abrupt change of topic, or includes content that is superficial or off-topic (for example, "I think you are too old to be crying"). Thus, the final code, *ratio of emotion coaching to emotion dismissing statements*, provided the relative balance of each type of response to the task and measured both quality and type of socialization around negative emotional events.

Results and Discussion. Data were analyzed separately by emotion type using correlational analyses and multivariate analyses of variance (MANOVAs) with child gender, parent gender, and age group as independent variables. See Table 5.2 for correlations among interaction task codes. See Tables 5.3 and 5.5 for sadness and anger MANOVA findings, respectively, and Tables 5.4 and 5.6 for means and standard deviations for significant pairwise comparisons.

Comparison of Sadness to Anger Discussions. Overall, the anger discussions were longer than the sadness discussions. The proportion of coaching to dismissing statements was higher for anger than for sadness discussions. It may be that it takes more parental "work" to socialize appropriate anger expression than it does for sadness. That is, there is likely more latitude for variations in sadness expression than there is for anger.

NEW DIRECTIONS FOR CHILD and ADOLESCENT DEVELOPMENT • DOI: 10.1002/cd

Table 5.2. Correlation Matrix for Interaction Task Codes for Conversations About Sadness and Anger

	M (SD)	1	2	3	4	5	6	7	8	9
Sadness										
Total words	126.12 (49.80)									
Proportion words—Parent	55.85 (17.41)	.15								
Negative emotion words—Parent	3.91 (3.23)	.53***	.60***							
Proportion of negative emotion words—Parent	72.10 (24.50)	−.34***	.19*	.37***						
Ratio of emotion coaching/emotion dismissing	2.34:1 (1.70)	−.32**	−.14	−.25**	−.03					
Anger										
Total words	182.36 (66.80)	.40***	.38***	.44***	−.01	−.26**				
Proportion words—Parent	61.10 (17.75)	.16	.27***	.29**	.21*	−.19*	.29**			
Negative emotion words—Parent	5.03 (3.58)	.36***	.53***	.59***	.14	−.18	.49***	.59***		
Proportion of negative emotion words—Parent	68.22 (26.87)	.01	.23*	.23*	.10	.11	.22*	.01	.50***	
Ratio of emotion coaching/emotion dismissing	3.39:1 (1.94)	−.19*	−.13	−.20*	−.06	.61***	−.29**	−.38***	−.30**	.01

Note. $* p < .05$, $** p < .01$, $*** p < .001$; t-test results for total words, $t(109) = 5.98$, $p < .001$; t-test results for ratio of emotion coaching/emotion dismissing, $t(109) = 6.34$, $p < .001$.

Table 5.3. Multivariate Analysis of Variance: Sadness Discussions

Dependent variable	Independent variable	df	F	η_p^2
Length of discussion	Child Gender × Age	1, 99	3.68*	.04
Proportion of words by	Parent Gender × Child Gender	1, 99	20.97***	.18
parents	Child Gender × Age	1, 99	81.33***	.45
	Parent Gender × Age	1, 99	33.93***	.26
Number of negative emotion	Parent Gender × Child Gender	1, 99	5.20*	.05
words	Child Gender × Age	1, 99	9.63**	.09
	Parent Gender × Age	1, 99	11.50***	.10
Ratio of emotion coaching to dismissing comments	Parent gender	1, 99	14.56***	.13

Note. $*p < .05$, $**p < .01$, $***p < .001$.

Sadness Findings. Inspection of conversations about sadness revealed several factors associated with parental coaching regardless of parent or child gender. Specifically, the longer the sadness discussion, the less the conversation comprised coaching elements. Further, the more that negative emotion words were used by parents in the discussion, the less the discussion reflected a coaching style. In addition, the more the parents led the discussion about sadness, the fewer coaching to dismissing statements were made. For boys and girls, it appears that there may be an optimal length of discussion for sadness-evoking events in which more discussion does not necessarily yield a better result in terms of positive, coaching types of behaviors that have previously been linked to adaptive emotional outcomes (Gottman et al., 1996).

Proportion of Words by Parents. For daughters only, fathers spoke for a greater proportion of the time compared to mothers whereas there was no difference for sons. Likewise, for younger children only, fathers spoke for a greater proportion of the time compared to mothers. It is possible that fathers may be less comfortable discussing sadness in general and prefer to exert greater control in conversations with children perceived to exhibit more overt sadness (for example, daughters and younger children). Perhaps reflective of the relative difference in perceived vulnerability to sadness, mothers and fathers led more of the conversation with younger compared to older boys, and with older girls than older boys.

Number of Negative Emotion Words. For girls only, fathers used negative emotion words in their discussions of sadness significantly more than mothers. For younger children only, fathers used negative emotion words significantly more than mothers in sadness discussions. It appears that fathers may be trying to respond to younger children and girls' sadness discussions by expanding on the emotion labeling aspects of their conversations with daughters. That is, fathers appear to be honing in on specific emotion labels (sad, disappointed, and others) that describe the

Table 5.4. Sadness Discussions: Significant Pairwise Comparisons

Dependent variable	Independent variable	Significant pairs	M	SD	t Value
Length of discussion	Child Gender × Age	Younger girls	147.29	64.70	
		Younger boys	111.76	46.32	2.39*
Proportion of words by parents (%)	Parent Gender × Child Gender	Fathers and daughters	72.71	8.52	10.24***
		Mothers and daughters	49.09	9.54	
	Child Gender × Age	Younger boys	61.06	12.89	
		Younger girls	51.07	17.77	2.44*
		Older boys	42.30	9.04	
		Older girls	69.19	16.24	7.65***
	Parent Gender × Age	Fathers and younger children	69.36	8.46	
		Mothers and younger children	43.66	11.20	9.34***
Number of negative emotion words	Parent Gender × Child Gender	Fathers and daughters	6.89	4.02	
		Mothers and daughters	2.62	2.46	4.85***
	Child Gender × Age	Older girls	5.20	2.65	
		Older boys	2.12	1.01	5.50***
	Parent Gender × Age	Fathers and younger children	6.84	4.24	
		Mothers and younger children	1.96	3.14	4.80***
Ratio of emotion coaching to dismissing comments	Parent gender	Mothers	2.95:1	1.88:1	3.97***
		Fathers	1.73:1	1.22:1	

Note. *p < .05, **p < .01, ***p < .001.

Table 5.5. Multivariate Analysis of Variance: Anger Discussions

Dependent variable	Independent variable	df	F	η_p^2
Proportion of words by parents	Parent Gender × Child Gender × Age	1, 99	8.82**	.08
Number of negative emotion words	Child Gender × Age	1, 99	23.09***	.19
Ratio of emotion coaching to dis-missing comments	Child gender	1, 99	5.73**	.05
	Parent gender	1, 99	15.78***	.13

Note. **p < .01, ***p < .001.

sadness-evoking event. This type of strategy, particularly with the younger children, may be a more rudimentary form of emotion socialization because it focuses on a basic competency of emotion identification in comparison to more advanced emotion coaching types.

Ratio of Emotion Coaching to Emotion Dismissing Comments. Mothers tended to use more coaching types of responses to their children than did fathers when discussing sadness. This finding is consistent with other research that has found children perceive their fathers to respond to their sadness with minimizing, ignoring, or neglecting types of responses, whereas mothers tend to be viewed as using problem-focused and encouraging types of strategies (Cassano et al., 2007; Garside & Klimes-Dougan, 2003).

Anger Findings. Inspection of conversations about anger furthers the notion that longer conversations are not necessarily better conversations when discussing negative emotion. Specifically, shorter conversations tended to contain the most parental coaching. In addition, parents who used more negative emotion words during a conversation about anger engaged in less coaching responses. Taken together with a similar pattern in conversations about sadness, it seems plausible that when parents provide less coaching, emotion-related discussions take longer to reach a sense of conclusion or resolution. As a result, these findings suggest that longer conversations may not necessarily provide children with an enhanced socialization experience.

Proportion of Words by Parents. For older children only, mothers spoke for a significantly greater proportion of the time to their daughters compared to their sons. There were no significant findings for younger children, and no differences were seen in conversations that involved fathers. It may be that mothers are more aware of gender role socialization pressures for anger and feel responsible for teaching their daughters how to modify their anger expression in accord with societal expectations. This awareness may lead to a tendency to take charge of opportunities for direct socialization.

Number of Negative Emotion Words. Parents used negative emotion words more frequently with younger than older boys. It may be

Table 5.6. Anger Discussions: Significant Pairwise Comparisons

Dependent variable	Independent variable	Significant variables	M	SD	t Value
Proportion of words by parents (%)	Parent Gender × Child Gender × Child Age	Mothers and older girls	79.72	9.81	
		Mothers and older boys	40.29	5.39	12.80***
Number of negative emotion words	Child Gender × Age	Older boys	5.11	3.74	
		Younger boys	1.12	2.91	4.35***
Ratio of emotion coaching to dis- missing comments	Child gender	Boys	3.90:1	2.14:1	
		Girls	2.98:1	1.64:1	2.54***
	Parent gender	Mothers	3.90:1	2.14:1	
		Fathers	2.71:1	1.50:1	3.98***

Note. ***p < .001.

that parents are teaching one of the fundamental aspects of competence, emotion labeling, with their younger boys in an effort to assist their development. By labeling the affective experience, they may be facilitating the acquisition and consolidation of their sons' emotion lexicon, which may assist in later regulation efforts.

Ratio of Emotion Coaching to Emotion Dismissing Comments. Consistent with a body of literature indicating that boys receive more instructive socialization of anger than girls (for example, Fivush, 1989), mothers used a higher proportion of coaching to dismissing responses with sons than for daughters. Further, mothers had a higher ratio of coaching to dismissing comments compared to fathers. This finding is again consistent with the aforementioned literature documenting that mothers seem to be more frequent coaches during socialization opportunities compared to fathers.

Conclusions

Overall, these results aptly illustrate the complexity that underlies emotion socialization processes by demonstrating the ways in which parent and child gender interact to produce different emotion experiences. Further, there does not seem to be one variable that is predominately influential; parent gender, child gender, child age, and type of emotion all appear to make important contributions to socialization processes and the development and refinement of ER skills. One of the novel aspects of this study is the designation of parent gender as an independent variable. Findings indicate that mothers adopted an emotion coaching approach more than fathers did regardless of the emotion being discussed. Fathers appear to play an especially unique role with sadness socialization, reflected in how much they controlled the conversation particularly with daughters and younger children and used more negative emotion words in sadness conversations, especially with younger children. Fathers' use of negative emotion words was related to fewer coaching types of responses. Taken together, these findings are consistent with previous research documenting mothers are more likely than fathers to provide children with socialization responses that promote adaptive regulation of sadness (Cassano et al., 2007; Garside & Klimes-Dougan, 2003).

Mothers' emotion socialization is distinctly captured in their conversations about anger. Mothers were observed to be directive in the anger conversations, particularly with older daughters. Although speculative, it seems plausible that mothers are more aware than fathers of the cultural importance and negative consequences associated with anger expressivity by females. Interestingly, parents coached their sons more than daughters; this finding dovetails with other research that found that mothers displayed more positive emotional responses to their preschool age sons' anger displays than their daughters' anger expressivity (Cole, Teti, & Zahn-Waxler, 2003). Based on our findings using a middle childhood sample, it appears that some aspects of parental emotion socialization are continued into the middle childhood years. Future research could help explain whether these continuities represent stability in particular emotion and/or gender socialization goals (e.g., promoting anger inhibition among daughters). Likewise, additional research is needed that evaluates links between parental socialization and the development of ER skills in middle childhood.

Ample research has pointed to the complexity of parental socialization of younger children, but we know considerably less about socialization processes in middle childhood (see Thompson & Meyer, 2007 for a review). The interesting set of findings that emerged from our middle childhood sample clearly highlights the salience of parental emotion socialization practices beyond the preschool period. Although parent-child emotion socialization histories are well established by middle childhood (Zeman & Garber, 1996), data from our study indicate that parent-child emotion discussions continue to be an important aspect in children's emotional development, perhaps through refining, modifying, and consolidating emotion processes such as emotional understanding, emotional self-efficacy, and facets related to emotional self-regulation. It is possible that parental socialization during middle childhood helps facilitate children's transition and adjustment to the emotional demands of adolescence. Clearly, more research is needed to better understand the specific social and psychological benefits accrued from emotion-focused conversations and the underlying mechanisms that facilitate adaptive emotion development.

Parent-child discussions provide a unique window into parental emotion socialization, as illustrated by our study. A rich set of findings emanated from the use of a relatively simple task with open-ended instructions designed to closely resemble actual conversations between parents and children. Future research should develop methods of validating parent-child discussion tasks to determine their relevance to discussions that occur in naturalistic environments. Interestingly, Leaper, Anderson, and Sanders (1998) noted in their meta-analysis of parents' talk with their children that differences due to parent gender were larger when the discussions were held in the home versus a lab setting, and when an unstructured activity was used rather than a concrete, narrowly defined problem-solving task. In addition, in our study, we had parents discuss both sadness and anger experiences with their children, which expands our understanding of parent and child differences in emotion discussions. In particular, asking parents and children to discuss specific emotions extends previous research in which parents tended to discuss sadness with girls but anger with boys (Fivush et al., 2000). In a field plagued by a dearth of validated assessment instruments (Zeman, Klimes-Dougan, Cassano, & Adrian, 2007), parent-child discussions may offer invaluable insight into processes that contribute to adaptive ER throughout development.

Limitations and Future Directions. From the evidence provided by this study, ample justification exists for conducting additional research on emotion socialization processes in middle childhood that also incorporates fathers into the design. It would also be valuable to include all parenting figures (for example, stepparents, grandparents), as well as siblings, from a household in the study design to explore their contributions to the emotion socialization process. Further, it would be interesting to investigate how parental emotion philosophies may be related to perceptions and observations of children's ER abilities and behaviors. There is a need for more standardized observational designs that can promote and facilitate comparison across different studies, as methodological differences shape (and limit) what theoretical conclusions one can draw. One of the limitations of the current research was the sample's homogeneity that potentially limited the generalizability of our findings. Clearly, as emotion socialization processes may differ by social and cultural contexts (Saarni, 1998), these variables should be incorporated into future research efforts. Lastly, there is a need to examine psychosocial outcomes of different socialization strategies implemented by mothers and fathers. It is not enough to know that fathers and mothers employ unique approaches to emotion socialization; rather, what is the short- and long-term impact of these approaches to psychosocial adaptation?

The evidence summarized in our chapter points to the conclusion that socialization of emotion is a transactional process. Specifically, recent trends in emotion socialization literature suggest a need to reconsider parents and children as both socializing agents and emotion regulators. It may be that processes that lead to gender-stereotyped emotional behavior are a sort of self-fulfilling prophecy by providing behavioral and emotional consequences for parents and children. In other words, parents' own affective reactions to children's emotional expressivity are likely driven by internalized gender-based expectations that reflect their own socialization history. When given an opportunity to socialize emotions, parents may experience emotions that are based on previous parent-child reactions, as well as by their beliefs and attitudes about appropriate and adaptive emotional behavior. It follows that the way parents manage their own cognitive and emotional reactions impacts socialization behavior that in turn is shaped by their child's ongoing emotional development and patterns of expressivity and regulation. Further, because socialization histories of parents are likely to have fallen in line with traditional gender norms, the influence of parents' cognition, affect, and behavior during socialization may conspire to perpetuate gender stereotypes in future generations. Although largely descriptive, the current chapter highlights variables that guide developmental trajectories of children and the importance of considering parents and children as co-socializers of gender-based emotion regulation. In addition to underscoring the importance of considering parent gender, child gender, and emotion type as core determinants of emotional development, it is our hope that this chapter facilitates and encourages greater refinement of our understanding of parents and children in the co-socialization of emotion.

References

Adams, S., Kuebli, K., Boyle, P.A., & Fivush, R. (1995). Gender differences in parent-child conversations about past emotions: A longitudinal investigation. *Sex Roles, 33,* 309–323.

Bretherton, I., Fritz, J., & Zahn-Waxler, C. (1986). Learning to talk about emotions: A functionalist perspective. *Child Development, 57,* 529–548.

Cassano, M., Adrian, M., Veits, G., & Zeman, J. (2006). The inclusion of fathers in the empirical investigation of child psychopathology: An update. *Journal of Clinical Child and Adolescent Psychology, 35,* 583–589.

Cassano, M., Zeman, J., & Perry-Parrish, C. (2007). Influence of gender on parental socialization of children's sadness regulation. *Social Development, 16,* 210–231.

Cervantes, C.A., & Callanan, M.A. (1998). Labels and explanations in mother-child emotion talk: Age and gender differentiation. *Developmental Psychology, 34,* 88–98.

Cole, P., Teti, L., & Zahn-Waxler, C. (2003). Mutual emotion regulation and the stability of conduct problems between preschool and early school age. *Development and Psychopathology, 15,* 1–18.

Denham, S.A. (1998). *Emotional development in young children.* New York: Guilford.

Dunn, J., Bretherton, I., & Munn, P. (1987). Conversations about feeling states between mothers and their young children. *Developmental Psychology, 23,* 132–139.

Eisenberg, N., Spinrad, T. L., & Cumberland, A. (1998). Parental socialization of emotion. *Psychological Inquiry, 9,* 241–273.

Fivush, R. (1989). Exploring sex differences in the emotional content of mother-child conversations about the past. *Sex Roles, 20,* 675–691.

Fivush, R., Brotman, M., Buckner, J., & Goodman, S. (2000). Gender differences in parent-child emotion narratives. *Sex Roles, 42,* 233–253.

Garside, R.B., & Klimes-Dougan, B. (2003). Socialization of discrete negative emotions: Gender differences and links with psychological distress. *Sex Roles, 47,* 115–128.

Gordon, S.L. (1989). The socialization of children's emotions: Emotional culture, competence, and exposure. In C. Saarni & P. L. Harris (Eds.), *Children's understanding of emotion* (pp. 319–349). New York: Cambridge University Press.

Gottman, J. M., Katz, L. F., & Hooven, C. (1996). Parental meta-emotion philosophy and the emotional life of families: Theoretical models and preliminary data. *Journal of Family Psychology, 10,* 243–268.

Halberstadt, A. G., Denham, S. A., & Dunsmore, J. C. (2001). Affective social competence. *Social Development, 10,* 79–119.

Klimes-Dougan, B., & Zeman, J. (2007). Introduction to the special issue of *Social Development*: Emotion socialization in childhood and adolescence. *Social Development, 16,* 203–209.

Leaper, C., Anderson, K. J., & Sanders, P. (1998). Moderators of gender effects on parents' talk to their children: A meta-analysis. *Developmental Psychology, 34,* 3–27.

Lunkenheimer, E. S., Shields, A. M., & Cortina, K. S. (2007). Parental emotion coaching and dismissing in family interaction. *Social Development, 16,* 232–248.

Lytton, H., & Romney, D. M. (1991). Parents' differential socialization of boys and girls: A meta-analysis. *Psychological Bulletin, 109*, 267–296.

Maccoby, E. E. (1990). Gender and relationships: A developmental account. *American Psychologist, 45*, 513–520.

Maccoby, E. E. (1998). *The two sexes: Growing up apart, growing together.* Cambridge, MA: Harvard University Press.

McDowell, D. J., Kim, M., O'Neil, J., & Parke, R. D. (2002). Children's emotional regulation and social competence in middle childhood: The role of maternal and paternal interactive style. *Marriage and Family Review, 34*, 345–364.

McDowell, D. J., O'Neil, R., & Parke, R. D. (2000). Display rule application in a disappointing situation and children's emotional reactivity: Relations with social competence. *Merrill-Palmer Quarterly, 46*, 306–324.

Saarni, C. (1984). An observational study of children's attempts to monitor their expressive behavior. *Child Development, 55*, 1504–1513.

Saarni, C. (1998). Issues of cultural meaningfulness in emotional development. *Developmental Psychology, 34*, 647–652.

Saarni, C. (1999). *The development of emotional competence.* New York: Guilford Press.

Siegal, M. (1987). Are sons and daughters treated more differently by fathers than by mothers? *Developmental Review, 7*, 183–209.

Sroufe, L. A. (2005). Attachment and development: A prospective, longitudinal study from birth to adulthood. *Attachment and Human Development, 7*, 349–367.

Thompson, R. A. (1990). Emotion and self-regulation. In R. A. Thompson (Ed.), *Nebraska symposium on motivation: Vol. 36. Socioemotional development* (pp. 367–467). Lincoln: University of Nebraska Press.

Thompson, R. A., & Meyer, S. (2007). Socialization of emotion regulation in the family. In J. Gross (Ed.), *Handbook of emotion regulation* (pp. 249–268). New York: Guilford Press.

Zeman, J., & Garber, J. (1996). Display rules for anger, sadness, and pain: It depends on who is watching. *Child Development, 67*, 957–973.

Zeman, J., Klimes-Dougan, B., Cassano, M., & Adrian, M. (2007). Measurement issues in emotion research with children and adolescents. *Clinical Psychology: Science and Practice, 14*, 377–401.

Zeman, J., & Shipman, K. (1996). Children's expression of negative affect: Reasons and methods. *Developmental Psychology, 32*, 842–849.

JANICE ZEMAN *is an associate professor in the department of psychology at the College of William and Mary. Her program of research examines emotion regulation processes in childhood and adolescence with particular emphases on (a) parental and peer socialization of anger and sadness; (b) the role of emotion regulation in the development, maintenance, and exacerbation of internalizing symptomatology; and (c) the assessment of emotion in children.*

CARISA PERRY-PARRISH *is a postdoctoral fellow at Johns Hopkins University School of Medicine, Division of General Pediatrics and Adolescent Medicine. Her research examines the roles of gender, ethnicity, and social context in the associations between emotion regulation and psychosocial functioning in children and adolescents.*

MICHAEL CASSANO *is a postdoctoral fellow at the Center for Management of ADHD at the Children's Hospital of Philadelphia. His research interests include parental socialization of children's emotion regulation abilities, behavioral health screening in pediatric primary care centers, and multisystemic treatment of ADHD.*

Brand, A. E., & Klimes-Dugan, B. (2010). Emotion socialization in adolescence: The roles of mothers and fathers. In A. Kennedy Root & S. Denham (Eds.), *The role of gender in the socialization of emotion: Key concepts and critical issues. New Directions for Child and Adolescent Development, 128*, 85–100. San Francisco: Jossey-Bass.

6

Emotion Socialization in Adolescence: The Roles of Mothers and Fathers

Ann E. Brand, Bonnie Klimes-Dougan

Abstract

This chapter provides a review of the literature that examines the role of mothers and fathers in socializing emotion in their sons and daughters during adolescence. Within the context of this chapter, we focus on mother-father similarities, differences, and coordinated efforts in socializing the emotion of their adolescent children. Empirical data is presented that provides new evidence about the coordinated efforts of parents and its implications for the development of adolescent psychopathology. The authors emphasize the importance of both adolescent emotion capabilities and the role mothers and fathers play in supporting or deterring healthy emotional development in adolescence. © Wiley Periodicals, Inc.

As a species, humans are emotional creatures. Thought to be largely biologically driven processes that evolve over time (Tomkins & McCarter, 1964 as summarized by Ekman, 1984), emotions serve as adaptive functions throughout the lifespan of an individual (Izard, 1991; Tomkins, 1962, 1963). There is also substantial evidence for the role of environmental influences in modifying the expression of emotion. A variety of environmental factors, including caretakers, teachers, peers, and society at large (for example, media), is likely to influence emotional expression through adolescence. Parents are one of the initial, and potentially most influential, sources by which children's emotions are socialized (Halberstadt, 1991). Despite an individual's move toward autonomy in adolescence, parents likely remain an important influence in the emotional lives of their adolescent children (Larson et al., 1996). The manner in which mothers and fathers coordinate their approach to emotions in their adolescent children has implications for the development of adolescent psychopathology.

The goal of this chapter is to examine the role of mothers and fathers in socializing emotion in their sons and daughters during adolescence. Within the context of this chapter, we will focus on mother-father similarities, differences, and coordinated efforts in socializing the emotions of their adolescent children. These efforts are thought to be critical to understanding how parents can support or deter healthy development during adolescence.

Emotion Socialization in Adolescence

Although the foundation for child emotion regulation is largely in place by middle childhood, it is critically important to understand how parental practices continue to influence emotion regulation into adolescence (see the special issue of *Social Development* edited by Klimes-Dougan and Zeman, 2007). Parenting practices are likely to be affected by the biological changes that take place in adolescents. These changes include reorganization of the frontal-limbic neurocircuitry and neurobiological stress systems implicated in emotional processing (reviewed by Zeman, Klimes-Dougan, Cassano, & Adrian, 2007). Adolescents face new social challenges as they interact more frequently with peers, place a higher premium on friendships and social acceptance, and begin to face the challenges associated with the development and maintenance of romantic relationships (Larson et al., 1996; Steinberg & Silk, 2002). At the same time, the demands for adherence to cultural norms and standards also increase. Parents expect more emotionally competent behavior with increasing child age, and therefore alter their expectations (Cassano, Perry-Parrish, & Zeman, 2007; Dix, 1991; O'Neal & Malatesta-Magai, 2005) and emotion socialization practices accordingly. For example, they may tend to be less supportive or more punitive with older children than younger children

NEW DIRECTIONS FOR CHILD and ADOLESCENT DEVELOPMENT • DOI: 10.1002/cd

(Dix, 1991; Klimes-Dougan et al., 2007; Lukenheimer, Sheilds, & Cortina, 2007). As adolescents proceed with establishing autonomy, emotion coaching practices that were of critical importance in early childhood (Gottman, Katz, & Hooven, 1997) may give way to alternative practices. It may be important for parents to model emotion regulation for older children (Katz & Hunter, 2007). Collectively, these emotionally evocative developmental tasks potentially tax both the adolescent's and his or her parents' abilities to regulate the strong emotions that typically accompany adolescence. However, these tasks also provide important opportunities for parents to aid their adolescent child in acquiring strategies for managing his or her own emotions.

Theories of Emotion Socialization. Parents are faced with the daunting task of guiding their children to conform to societal standards. In the face of such standards and perceived requirements, parents use indirect (social referencing, modeling, overall affective environment) and direct (coaching/teaching, discussing emotions, contingencies for emotional behavior) socialization practices to shape the emotional lives of their offspring during childhood and continuing through much of adolescence (see Chapter One; Andersen & Guerrero, 1998; Saarni, 1985, 1993).

Irrespective of whether the method of emotion socialization is indirect or direct, socializing parents may foster or inhibit the expression of emotion. Early on, Tomkins (1962, 1963) identified specific behaviors for enhancing emotion regulation in offspring that include acknowledging, attending to, and helping the child cope with negative emotions. He also suggested that dampening children's negative affect by utilizing strategies that deemphasize, rather than strengthen, negative emotions is desirable. Gottman et al. (1997) and Eisenberg, Cumberland, and Spinrad (1998) have extended this work to identify key parental approaches (for example, emotion coaching, emotion-related socialization behaviors) that facilitate child emotional competence. Finally, other models of emotion socialization stress the importance of discrete emotions. Malatesta-Magai et al. (Malatesta-Magai, 1991; Malatesta & Wilson, 1988) delineated strategies that parents commonly use to directly socialize their children's discrete negative emotions, including strategies that presumably facilitate or interfere with the child's ability to regulate sadness, anger, and shame. Applications of these emotion socialization theories are evident in research with adolescents.

Parental Similarities in Emotion Socialization. In many regards, mothers and fathers use similar approaches to socializing emotion in their sons and daughters. Although providing empirical evidence for the null hypothesis poses considerable challenges, some evidence for similarities in parenting approaches is descriptively provided here. Research with both children and adolescents has noted similar emotion socialization responses for mothers and fathers (McDowell et al., 2002). For example,

Aldrich and Tennenbaum (2006) found that mothers and fathers do not differ in the number of emotion words used when discussing hypothetical situations with their adolescent children. Similarities between parents have also been noted with regard to discrete emotions. Mothers and fathers often express both similar types of emotions and more positive than negative emotions within the family (Garside, 2004; Halberstadt, 1991). Adolescent and young adult participants endorsed punishing emotional displays as the least common response and encouraging an open dialogue about emotions as the most common response for both parents (Garside & Klimes-Dougan, 2002; Klimes-Dougan et al., 2007).

Parental Differences in Emotion Socialization. Despite the aforementioned similarities, there are also potentially important differences in parental emotion socialization practices. Dramatic changes in family structure over the past several decades include women increasingly assuming provider status in the family. Nevertheless, mothers continue to be primarily responsible for child rearing. Furthermore, contemporary research continues to show that mothers are more involved than fathers in parenting their adolescent children (Paulson & Sputa, 1996). Reporting to be more emotionally expressive than fathers within the context of family relationships, mothers provide opportunities for modeling emotional expressiveness (Halberstadt et al., 1995). Emotional labeling and understanding may also be more likely to be learned in mother-child interactions. For example, conversations between mothers and children regarding emotional experiences were significantly longer than conversations with fathers (Fivush et al., 2000). Mothers, more than fathers, have been found to use emotion coaching with their school-age children (Cassano et al., 2007; Gottman et al., 1997). Research on adolescents and emerging adults (Garside, 2004; Garside & Klimes-Dougan, 2002; Klimes-Dougan et al., 2007) has consistently noted that mothers rewarded and magnified displays of sadness, fear, and anger more than fathers. Fathers were more likely to overlook or ignore their adolescent's expressions of negative emotions.

Despite the lower levels of involvement, the father's role may be pivotal in shaping the emotional displays of their adolescent children. Although the focus of fathers' socialization responses with their adolescent offspring is sparse, the broader developmental literature may be informative. For example, Parke (1996) noted that father-child interactions are characterized by greater emotional arousal as well as more unpredictability, and has argued that this provides greater opportunities for learning emotion regulatory skills within the context of these exchanges. Father's emotion socialization practices predicted child emotional competence (McDowell & Parke, 2005) and psychological distress (Garside, 2004). Also, fathers are often more punitive in response to their children's displays of emotion than mothers (Cassano et al., 2007; Eisenburg, Fabes, & Murphy, 1996). Klimes-Dougan et al. (2007) found that fathers

New Directions for Child and Adolescent Development • DOI: 10.1002/cd

were more likely than mothers to use dismissive or distracting strategies to respond to their child's expression of fear or sadness. When fathers use emotion coaching practices with their children, they are more likely to coach anger than sadness (Gottman et al., 1997).

Perhaps in an effort to provide critical feedback about functional sex-role emotional behaviors (Zahn-Waxler, 2000), fathers tend to be more differentiated than mothers in their parenting practices with their sons and daughters (for reviews, see Lytton & Romney, 1991; Siegal, 1987). In many cultures, there are expectations that men should not express emotion, particularly vulnerable or intropunitive emotions such as sadness or fear, for these may be interpreted as a sign of weakness. For example, fathers reportedly rewarded their daughters and punished their sons for expressing sadness and fear (Garside & Klimes-Dougan, 2002).

It is beyond the scope of this chapter to fully examine how parents socialize their sons and daughters (see Zahn-Waxler, 2000), yet together, these findings indicate that the influence of gender for both the parent and child are important in understanding the process by which emotions are socialized. Overall, the findings on mother-father emotion socialization practices suggest that the differences that emerge may be critical in shaping emotional behavior in sons and daughters.

Maternal-Paternal Consistency in Emotion Socialization with Adolescent Children. It is not only important to consider similarities and differences in parental emotion socialization practices, but it is also critical to evaluate if mothers and fathers work together in parenting their adolescents. Past research conducted with a broader array of parenting practices is relevant to understanding coordinated efforts or consistency in emotion socialization practices of parents. The literature is mixed as to whether parental consistency regarding optimal parenting practices is necessary to buffer children from negative stressors or whether "one-good parent" is sufficient (Rutter, 1987). Some research offers support for the "one-good-parent" hypothesis, suggesting that parental consistency in child-rearing practices is not necessary for positive child adjustment as long as one parent provides optimal parenting (Fletcher, Steinberg, & Sellers, 1999; Katz & Gottman, 1995, 1997; Rutter, 1987; Ryan, Martin, & Brooks-Gunn, 2006). For example, Rutter (1987) reported that children who had a warm and uncritical relationship with at least one parent demonstrated lower levels of conduct disorder when compared with children who had no positive parental relationship. Yet, some studies have found support for the importance of parental consistency for positive adolescent adjustment. Wagner, Cohen, and Brook (1996) found that, under situations of stress, adolescents had fewer symptoms of depression if they perceived both parents as warm; adolescents had more symptoms of depression if they perceived one or neither parent as warm. Similarly, Johnson, Shulman, and Collins (1991) found that adolescent perceptions of discrepant parenting patterns, with only one parent practicing authoritative parenting, was associated with low self-esteem, poor school adaptation, and poor school achievement.

One consistent finding in the literature examining parental consistency is that two parents practicing poor parenting strategies is related to poor adolescent adjustment (Buchanan et al., 1996; Fletcher et al., 1999; Johnson et al., 1991; Wagner et al., 1996). For example, Fletcher et al. (1999) found that adolescents who perceived at least one parent to be authoritative had better academic competence than adolescents from homes with two nonauthoritative parents. Interestingly, adolescents faced with discrepant parenting, with only one parent perceived as authoritative, had more symptoms of psychological distress than those from consistent nonauthoritative homes. Still, the authors concluded that perceiving parents as consistent is less important than perceiving at least one parent to be authoritative.

Little research has been conducted exploring the importance of parental consistency in emotion socialization. Examining relations between parental meta-emotion philosophy and emotion coaching practices, Gottman et al. (1997) found fathers who were aware of their own sadness were not only more likely to coach emotion in their children, but were also more likely to have a wife who coached emotion as well. Further exploration of discrepancies in meta-emotion philosophies found that where there was a discrepancy, the father was less likely to be emotion coaching than the mother. Given the research supporting the relations between maternal meta-emotion philosophy and depressive symptomatology in adolescence (Katz & Hunter, 2007), further exploration of parental consistency in emotion socialization practices in adolescence is warranted.

Research Study: The Consistency of Parental Emotion Socialization Practices

In an unpublished dissertation, Brand (2001) examined the importance of parental consistency in emotion socialization practices by evaluating adolescents from two-parent families. Specifically, she examined whether the coordinated emotion socialization efforts of mothers and fathers were linked with the development of internalizing and externalizing problems in their adolescent children. As part of a larger, multimethod, longitudinal investigation conducted at the National Institute of Mental Health (Klimes-Dougan et al., 2001; Zahn-Waxler et al., 2001), participants in this study included 158 adolescents (79 male) with two parental figures living in the home. Youth ranged in age from 11 to 16, with a mean age of 13.05 ($SD = 1.58$), varied in their ethnicity (81.6% White, 5.7% Black, 0.6% Hispanic, 3.2% Asian, and 8.2% other), and were from well-educated, middle- to upper-middle class families. Because of the approach used to recruit participants, age and sex (respectively, 49% and 52% male in the low-risk and high-risk groups) distributions were comparable for the low-risk and high-risk groups.

The primary measures included the scales that assessed behavioral and emotional problems and emotion socialization. The internalizing and externalizing scales of the Child Behavior Checklist (CBCL) and the Youth Self-Report (YSR; Achenbach, 1991a, 1991b) were administered as well as the Emotions as a Child, Child Version 1.2 (EAC; Klimes-Dougan et al., 2001; Magai, 1996). The EAC was used to assess the adolescent's perception of the methods their mothers and fathers used to socialize anger and sadness, and yielded five emotion socialization strategies that included reward (providing comfort, and empathizing), punish (expressing disapproval or making fun of a child), override (dismissive or distracting parental behaviors), neglect (ignore a child's expression of emotion), and magnify (parental behaviors that match the expression of a child, such as a parent becoming fearful when their child shows fear). Results of factor analyses have suggested that reward and override are generally facilitative, supportive strategies (positive) in that they promote optimal emotion regulation. Neglect, punish, and magnify (for anger only) are strategies considered inhibiting, unsupportive, and punitive (negative). Based on median splits of the EAC scales, parents were classified as high or low on the positive and negative summary scales for each emotion. Parental pairs were placed into seven groups based on their socialization classification (see Table 6.1). Multiple regression techniques were used to examine the coordinated efforts of mothers and fathers in socializing the sadness and anger of their adolescents.

The pattern of results varied for each emotion, suggesting that the socialization of specific emotions may play a unique role in the presence of internalizing and externalizing symptoms in adolescents. Consistent with functional theories of emotion, frequent use by both parents of negative emotion socialization strategies was associated with higher levels of adolescent internalizing symptomatology (Groups 4, 5; Table 6.2). One

Table 6.1. Definition of Parental Groups

Group 1	Both parents high positive/low negative
Group 2	Only one parent high positive/low negative
Group 3	Both parents high positive/high negative
Group 4	One parent low positive/high negative and one parent high positive/high negative
Group 5	Both parents low positive/high negative
Group 6	One parent low positive/low negative and one parent low positive/high negative
Group 7	Both parents low positive/low negative

Table 6.2. Multiple Regression: Perceived Discrepancies in Parental Responses to Sadness and Adolescent Psychopathology

	CBCL Internalizing			YSR Internalizing		
	B	SE B	β	B	SE B	β
Group 1	48.45	1.55		45.87	1.86	
Group 2	4.45	2.18	.19*	4.21	2.62	.15
Group 3	-3.07	3.72	-.07	7.51	4.47	.14
Group 4	13.01	3.27	.33**	13.68	3.93	.29**
Group 5	4.55	2.49	.17	8.61	2.96	.27**
Group 6	.78	2.74	.03	8.92	3.23	.25**
Group 7	5.55	2.85	.17	5.38	3.42	.14

$F (6, 150) = 3.76**, R^2 = .13$ $\qquad$ $F (6, 150) = 3.09**, R^2 = .11$

Note. CBCL = Child Behavior Checklist; YSR = Youth Self-Report. Groups dummy-coded with Group 1 serving as the comparison group. Groups entered simultaneously. Group 1, $N = 38$; Group 2, $N = 39$; Group 3, $N = 8$, Group 4, $N = 11$; Group 5, $N = 25$, Group 6, $N = 19$; Group 7, $N = 16$. *$p < .05$, **$p < .01$.

exception was noted in the group of parents who were consistent in the frequent use of both positive and negative responses (Group 3). Also, infrequent use of positive strategies by both parents was associated with higher levels of adolescent internalizing symptomatology (Groups 6, 7).

Conversely, the socialization of anger was associated with both measures of internalizing and externalizing symptoms. This pattern of findings suggests that socialization practices may have a broad scope of influence, impacting the regulation of both anger as well as vulnerable emotions like sadness. Frequent use of negative strategies by both parents was associated with higher levels of adolescent internalizing and externalizing symptomatology (Groups 3, 4, 5; Table 6.3). Also, infrequent use of positive strategies by both parents was associated with higher levels of adolescent internalizing and externalizing symptomatology (Group 6). One exception was noted in the group of parents who were consistent in the infrequent use of both positive and negative responses (Group 7) in which no links with psychopathology were noted. In contrast to sadness, the use of frequent positive and infrequent negative responses by only one parent was also associated with higher levels of internalizing and externalizing symptomatology (Group 2). Although shared-respondent variance and cross-sectional design limit the implications of these results, the findings warrant attention for future research.

These findings support theories of emotion regulation, which postulate that parental socialization of emotion is central to the development of regulatory processes of emotion (Cole et al., 1994). Parental consistency in the use of negative responses to emotion was associated with elevated levels of adolescent psychopathology when contrasted with adolescents

Table 6.3. Multiple Regression: Perceived Discrepancies in Parental Responses to Anger and Adolescent Psychopathology: Youth Self-Report (YSR)

	YSR Internalizing			YSR Externalizing		
	B	SE B	B	B	SE B	β
Group 1	44.33	2.07		46.20	1.54	
Group 2	8.05	2.83	.28**	7.65	2.11	.35**
Group 3	8.94	3.37	.24**	8.74	2.52	.31**
Group 4	11.78	3.37	.32**	8.30	2.52	.29**
Group 5	11.67	2.92	.39**	9.30	2.18	.40**
Group 6	4.17	4.50	.08	9.05	3.36	.22**
Group 7	4.07	3.27	.11	.55	2.44	.02
	$F (6, 152) = 3.75**, R^2 = .13$			$F (6, 152) = 5.61**, R^2 = .18$		

Note. Groups dummy-coded with Group 1 serving as the comparison group. Groups entered simultaneously. Group 1, $N = 30$; Group 2, $N = 35$; Group 3, $N = 18$, Group 4, $N = 18$; Group 5, $N = 30$; Group 6, $N = 8$; Group 7, $N = 20$. $*p < .05$, $**p < .01$.

who perceive consistency across parents in optimal responses to emotion. Research has established that punitive responses to emotion are associated with poor social and emotional competence through the dysregulation of emotion (Eisenberg et al., 1996; Gottman et al., 1997). The current findings are unique in that they point to the potentially damaging effects of consistent exposure to punitive emotion socialization responses from both parents. For the emotion of anger, perceiving both parents as frequently using optimal socialization strategies was not enough to counter the detrimental effects of two parents who also employed punishing and neglectful responses (Group 3).

These results were generally consistent with a discrete emotions framework in which Malatesta and Wilson (1988) asserted that parental emotion socialization strategies contribute to the ways in which affective organizations develop and become consolidated over time, resulting in risk or adaptation. Each emotion has a specific function in the motivation and organization of behavior (Izard, 1991). In reaction to social interactions with parents, particular emotional states become increasingly reinforced in experience and internalized as part of the self. Certain emotion socialization practices may be implicated in the development of emotional and behavioral problems. The results here suggest that when parents do not facilitate the regulation of sadness, sadness in their adolescent children may become monopolistic and dominate personality, which may lead to moderate distortions that define personality or to more severe distortions found in internalizing psychopathology. This is particularly important to consider given the developmental tasks regarding personality formation present in adolescence.

The link between discrete emotion and the type of psychopathology manifested is not always straightforward. Discrepancies in parental responses to the expression of anger may play a role in the adolescent's regulation of vulnerable emotions such as sadness. Research indicates that children expect some differences in maternal and paternal responses to anger that may be considered typical (Fuchs & Thelen, 1988; Saarni, 1989). However, a great departure from these expectancies may contribute to the dysregulation of sadness due to mixed messages from parents regarding emotions. More so, results suggest that parental consistency in high levels of negative responses to anger may be particularly detrimental to the regulation of intropunative emotions. Other possible explanations suggest that perceived discrepancies in parental responses to anger may promote anger turned inward (Freud, [1917]1957). For example, if adolescents perceive their parents as consistently punitive in their response to the expression of anger, they may suppress the expression of anger to avoid aversive responses from their parents, and thus not develop effective ways to regulate anger. Research suggests that hostility directed inward and the suppression of anger is linked to depression (Baggio & Godwin, 1987; Kopper & Epperson, 1996). The relations between emotion regulation and parent emotion socialization are further complicated by the search for autonomy, presenting a unique challenge to understanding these processes in adolescence.

The results of this study are not able to fully inform causal pathways, but highlight the importance of considering the bidirectional relationship of parent and child. Furthermore, it will be important for future research with larger samples to examine if these patterns of consistent and discrepant emotion socialization efforts for mothers and fathers differ with regard to child outcomes (for example, is it adequate to have a supportive father?) and if consistency in emotion socialization efforts influence sons and daughters differently.

Conclusions: Implications for the Development of Psychopathology and Intervention

This selective review of the literature and the research findings serve to highlight critical maternal and paternal emotion socialization practices used in raising adolescents. The results indicate that emotion socialization practices of the mother and father are similar in some regards, differ in some regards, and serve in concert to provide the scaffolding with which emotion regulation strategies are consolidated. Although normative sex differences in parenting are pervasive in our culture, under conditions of risk, these parental practices may be instrumental in producing specific developmental pathways that lead to maladaptive psychological functioning. Parental support may buffer the challenges adolescents face regarding regulating negative emotion and managing emotional lability (Greene, 1990; Larson et al.,

1996). For example, the findings of Stocker, Richmond, and Rhoades (2007) indicated that parental emotional expressiveness and parental emotion coaching differentially were linked to internalizing and externalizing symptoms in their normative adolescent sample. Parents who are dismissive of their children's feelings, particularly their vulnerable emotions, may predispose their child to developing acting-out problems (Gottman et al., 1997). There is a growing body of literature linking parental emotion socialization practices with various aspects of child adaptation and maladaptation (Cicchetti, Ackerman, & Izard, 1995; Denham, 1993; Denham et al., 2000; Eisenberg et al., 1998; Gottman et al., 1997; Katz, Wilson, & Gottman, 1999; O'Neal & Malatesta-Magai, 2005; Saarni, 1993; Shipman, Schneider, & Sims, 2005; Yap, Allen, & Ladouceur, 2008; Zahn-Waxler, Klimes-Dougan, & Slattery, 2000). Although parental emotion socialization practices may shape child outcomes, the contentious behavior of adolescents is equally likely to alter the ways that even the most capable parent responds (Ge et al., 1995; Yap, Allen, Leve, & Katz, 2008). Furthermore, less capable parents and those suffering from mental illness, may find the process of dealing with the emotional upheaval of their adolescent overwhelming (Race & Brand, 2003) and may hinder their adolescent's efforts to establish effective emotion regulation capacities.

Translating the empirical findings on risk and adaptation to prevention and intervention efforts will be an important next step (Havinghurst, Harley, & Prior, 2004; Izard, 2002). Preventative interventions may be targeted at adolescents, their parents, and/or their educators. Worthwhile goals directed at parents may include (1) increasing understanding of normative progressions of emotional development in adolescence, (2) enhancing understanding and regulation of emotions in parents, and (3) acquiring skills that serve to facilitate parent emotion coaching (Izard, 2002; Wagner & Klimes-Dougan, 2002). Some adolescents would benefit from efforts directed at increasing the child's emotional repertoire within the context of a supportive parental relationship (Greenberg, Kusche, Cook, & Quamma; 1995; Greenberg & Beck, 1990; Stark et al., 1996). For others, distraction, redirection, and refocusing feelings and other cognitive behavioral approaches to intervention may be critical tools to enhancing emotion regulation (for example, Stark et al., 2008). The results of this review suggest that, optimally, interventions should involve both mothers and fathers, for both are likely to play influential and complimentary roles in shaping the emotional response capabilities of their children.

References

Achenbach, T. M. (1991a). *Manual for the Child Behavior Checklist/4–18 and 1991 Profile*. Burlington: University of Vermont Department of Psychiatry.

Achenbach, T. M. (1991b). *Manual for the Youth Self-Report and 1991 Profile*. Burlington: University of Vermont Department of Psychiatry.

Aldrich, N. J., & Tenenbaum, H. R. (2006). Sadness, anger, and frustration: Gendered patterns in early adolescents' and their parents' emotion talk. *Sex Roles, 55*, 775–785.

Andersen, P. A., & Guerrero, L. K. (1998). *Handbook of communication and emotions: Research, theory, applications, and context*. San Diego: Academic Press.

Baggio, M. K., & Godwin, W. H. (1987). Relation of depression to anger and hostility constructs. *Psychological Reports, 61*, 87–90.

Brand, A. E. (2001). The role of perceived discrepancies in parental emotion socialization practices in the relation between marital adjustment and adolescent psychopathology (Doctoral Dissertation, University of North Carolina at Chapel Hill, 2001). *Dissertation Abstracts International, 62*, 5363.

Buchanan, C. M., Maccoby, E. E., & Dornbusch, S. M. (1996). *Adolescents after divorce*. Cambridge, MA: Harvard University Press.

Cassano, M., Perry-Parrish, C., & Zeman, J. (2007). Influence of gender on parental socialization of children's sadness regulation. *Social Development, 16*, 210–231.

Cicchetti, D., Ackerman, B.P., & Izard, C.E. (1995). Emotions and emotion regulation in developmental psychopathology. *Development and Psychopathology, 7*, 1–10.

Cole, P. M., Michel, M. K., & Teti, L. O. (1994). The development of emotion regulation and dysregulation: A clinical perspective. In N. A. Fox (Ed.), *The development of emotion regulation: Biological and behavioral considerations*. Monographs of the Society for Research in Child Development, 59 (2–3, Serial No. 240).

Denham, S. (1993). Maternal emotional responsiveness and toddlers' social-emotional competence. *Journal of Child Psychology and Psychiatry, 34*, 715–728.

Denham, S. A., Workman, E., Cole, P. M., Weissbrod, C., Kendziora, K., & Zahn-Waxler, C. (2000). Prediction of externalizing behavior problems from early to middle childhood: The role of parental socialization and emotion expression. *Development and Psychopathology, 12*, 23–45.

Dix, T. (1991). The affective organization of parenting: Adaptive and maladaptive processes. *Psychological Bulletin, 110*, 3–25.

Eisenberg, N., Cumberland, A., & Spinrad, T. L. (1998). Parental socialization of emotion. *Psychological Inquiry, 9*, 241–273.

Eisenberg, N., Fabes, R. A., & Murphy, B. C. (1996). Parents' reactions to children's negative emotions: Relations to children's social competence and comforting behavior. *Child Development, 67*, 2227–2247.

Ekman, P. (1984). Expression and the nature of emotion. In K. Scherer & P. Ekman (Eds.), Approaches to emotion (pp. 319–343). Hillsdale, NJ: Lawrence Erlbaum.

Fivush, R., Brotman, M., Buckner, J., & Goodman, S. (2000). Gender differences in parent-child emotion narratives. *Sex Roles, 42*, 233–253.

Fletcher, A. C., Steinberg, L., & Sellers, E. B. (1999). Adolescents' well-being as a function of perceived interparental consistency. *Journal of Marriage and the Family, 61*, 599–610.

Freud, S. (1917/1957). Mourning and melancholia. In J. Strachey (Ed.), *The standard edition of the complete psychological works of Sigmund Freud* (pp. 237–260). Vol. 14. London: Hogarth Press.

Fuchs, D, & Thelen, M. H. (1988). Children's expected interpersonal consequences of communicating their affective state and reported likelihood of expression. *Child Development, 59*, 1314–1322.

Garside, R. B. (2004) Parental socialization of discrete positive and negative emotions: Implications for emotional functioning. (Doctoral dissertation, The Catholic University of America, 2003). *Dissertation Abstracts International, 65*, 4828.

Garside, R. B., & Klimes-Dougan, B. (2002). Socialization of discrete negative emotions: Sex differences and links with psychological distress. *Sex Roles, 47*, 115–128.

Ge, X., Conger, R.D., Lorenz, F.O., Shannahan, M., & Elder, G.E. (1995). Mutual influences in parent and adolescent psychological distress. *Developmental Psychopathology, 31*, 406–419.

Gottman, J. M., Katz, L. F., & Hooven, C. (1997). *Meta-emotion: How families communicate emotionally.* Hillsdale, NJ: Lawrence Erlbaum Associates.

Greene, A. L. (1990). Patterns of affectivity in the transition to adolescence. *Journal of Experimental Child Psychology, 50*, 340–356.

Greenberg, M., & Beck, A. T. (1990). Cognitive approaches to psychotherapy: Theory and therapy. In R. Plutchik & H. Kellerman (Eds.), *Emotion, psychopathology, and psychotherapy: Emotion: Theory, research, and experience, Vol. 5* (pp. 177–194). San Diego: Academic Press.

Greenberg, M. T., Kusche, C. A., Cook, E. T., & Quamma, J. P. (1995). Promoting emotional competence in school-aged children: The effects of the PATHS curriculum. *Development and Psychopathology, 7*, 117–136.

Halberstadt, A. G. (1991). Socialization of expressiveness: Family influences in particular and a model in general. In R. S. Feldman & B. Rime (Eds.), *Fundamentals of emotional expressiveness* (pp. 106–162). Cambridge: Cambridge University Press.

Halberstadt, A. G., Cassidy, J., Stifter, C. A., Parke, R. D., & Fox, N. A. (1995). Self-expressiveness within the family context: Psychometric support for a new measure. *Psychological Assessment, 7*, 93–103.

Havinghurst, S. S., Harley, A., & Prior, M. (2004). Building preschool children's emotional competence: A parenting program. *Early Education and Development, 15*, 423–448.

Izard, C. E. (1991). *The psychology of emotions.* New York: Plenum Press.

Izard, C. E. (2002). Translating emotion theory and research into preventive interventions. *Psychological Bulletin, 128*, 796–824.

Johnson, B. M., Shulman, S., & Collins, W. A. (1991). Systemic patterns of parenting as reported by adolescents: Developmental differences and implications for psychosocial outcomes. *Journal of Adolescent Research, 6*, 235–252.

Katz, L. F., & Gottman, J. M. (1995). Marital interaction and child outcomes: A longitudinal study of mediating and moderating processes. In Cicchetti, Toth, et al. (Eds.), *Emotion, cognition, and representation: Rochester Symposium on Developmental Psychopathology.* Rochester, NY: University of Rochester Press.

Katz, L. F., & Gottman, J. M. (1997). Buffering children from marital conflict and dissolution. *Journal of Clinical Child Psychology, 26*, 157–171.

Katz, L. F., & Hunter, E. C. (2007). Maternal meta-emotion philosophy and adolescent depressive symptomatology. *Social Development, 16*(2), 343–360.

Katz, L. F., Wilson, B., & Gottman, J. M. (1999). Meta-emotion philosophy and family adjustment: Making an emotional connection. In M. J. Cox & J. Brooks-Gunn (Eds.), *Conflict and cohesion in families: Causes and consequences* (pp. 131–165). New York: Erlbaum.

Klimes-Dougan, B., Hastings, P. D., Granger, D. A., Usher, B. A., & Zahn-Waxler, C. (2001). Adrenocortisol activity in at-risk and normally developing adolescents: Individual differences in salivary cortisol basal levels, diurnal variation, and response to social challenges. *Development & Psychopathology, 13*, 695–719.

Klimes-Dougan, B., Brand, A. E., Zahn-Waxler, C., Usher, B., Hastings, P. D., Kendziora, K., & Garside, R. B. (2007). Parental emotion socialization in adolescence: Differences in sex, age, and problem status. *Social Development, 16*(2), 326–342.

Klimes-Dougan, B., & Zeman, J. (2007). Introduction to the special issue: Emotion socialization for middle-childhood and adolescence. *Social Development, 16*, 203–209.

Kopper, B. A., & Epperson, D. L. (1996). The experience and expression of anger: Relationships with gender, gender role socialization, depression, and mental health functioning. *Journal of Consulting Psychology, 43*, 158–165.

Larson, R. W., Richards, M. H., Moneta, G., Holmbeck, G., & Duckett, E. (1996). Changes in adolescents' daily interactions with their families from ages 10 to 18: Disengagement and transformation. *Developmental Psychology, 32*, 744–754.

Lukenheimer, E. S., Sheilds, A. M., & Cortina, K. S. (2007). Parental emotion coaching and dismissing in family interaction. *Social Development, 16*, 232–248.

Lytton, H., & Romney, D. M. (1991). Parents' differential socialization of boys and girls: A meta-analysis. *Psychological Bulletin, 109*, 267–296.

Magai, C. M. (1996). Emotions as a Child Self-Rating Scale. Unpublished measure, Long Island University.

Malatesta, C. Z. & Wilson, A. (1988). Emotion cognition interaction in personality development: A discrete emotions, functionalist analysis. *British Journal of Social Psychology, 27*, 91–112.

Malatesta-Magai, C. (1991). Emotional socialization: Its role in personality and developmental psychopathology. In D. Cicchetti & S. L. Toth (Eds.), *Internalizing and externalizing expressions of dysfunction* (pp. 203–224). Hillsdale, NJ: Lawrence Erlbaum Associates.

McDowell, D. J., Kim, M., O'Neil, R., & Parke, R. D. (2002). Children's emotional regulation and social competence in middle childhood: The role of maternal and paternal interactive style. In Richard A. Fabes (Ed.). *Emotions and the Family* (pp. 345–364). New York: The Haworth Press, Inc.

McDowell, D. J., & Parke, R. D. (2005). Parental control and affect as predictors of children's display rule use and social competence with peers. *Social Development, 14*, 440–457.

O'Neal, C., & Malatesta-Magai, C. (2005). Do parents respond in different ways when children feel different emotions? The emotional context of parenting. *Development and Psychopathology, 17*, 467–487.

Parke, R. D. (1996). *Fatherhood.* Cambridge. Harvard University Press.

Paulson, S. E., & Sputa, C. L. (1996). Patterns of parenting during adolescence: Perceptions of adolescents and parents. *Adolescence, 31*, 369–381.

Race, E., & Brand, A. E. (2003, April). *Parental personality and its relationship to socialization of sadness in children.* Poster presented at the biennial meeting of the Society for Research in Child Development, Tampa, FL.

Rutter, M. (1987). Psychosocial resilience and protective mechanisms. *American Journal of Orthopsychiatry, 57*, 316–331.

Ryan, R. M., Martin, A., & Brooks-Gunn, J. (2006). Is one parent good enough? Patterns of mother and father parenting and child cognitive outcomes at 24 and 6 months. *Parenting: Science & Practice, 6*, 211–228.

Saarni, C. (1985). Indirect processes in affect socialization. In M. Lewis and C. Saarni (Eds.). *The socialization of emotions* (pp. 187–209). New York: Plenum.

Saarni, C. (1989). Children's understanding of strategic control of emotional expression in social transactions. In C. Saarni & P. L. Harris (Eds.), *Children's understanding of emotion: Cambridge studies in social and emotional development* (pp. 181–208). New York: Cambridge University Press.

Saarni, C. (1993). Socialization of emotions. In M. Lewis & J. M. Haviland (Eds.), *Handbook of emotions* (pp. 435–446). New York: Guilford Press.

Shipman, K., Schneider, R., & Sims, C. (2005). Emotion socialization in maltreating and nonmaltreating mother-child dyads: Implications for children's adjustment. *Journal of Clinical Child and Adolescent Psychology, 34*, 590–596.

Siegal, M. (1987). Are sons and daughters treated more differently by fathers than by mothers? *Developmental Review, 7*, 183–209.

Stark, K. D., Napolitano, S., Swearer, S., Schmidt, K., Jaramilo, D., & Hoyle, J. (1996). Issues in the treatment of depressed children. *Applied and Preventative Psychology, 5*, 59–83.

Stark, K. D., Hargrave, J., Hersh, B., Greenberg, M., Fisher, M., & Herren, J. (2008). Treatment of youth depression: The ACTION program. In J. R. S. Abela & B. L. Hankin (Eds.), *Child and adolescent depression: Causes, treatment and prevention* (pp. 224–229). New York: Guilford.

Steinberg, L., & Silk, J. S. (2002). Parenting adolescents. In M. H. Bornstein, (Ed), *Handbook of parenting: Vol. 1: Children and parenting* (pp. 103–133). Mahwah, NJ: Lawrence Erlbaum Associates.

Stocker, C. M., Richmond, M. K., & Rhoades, G. K. (2007). Family emotional processes and adolescents' adjustment. *Social Development, 16,* 310–325.

Tomkins, S. S. (1962). *Affect, imagery, consciousness, Vol. I. The positive affects.* New York: Springer.

Tomkins, S.S. (1963). *Affect, imagery, consciousness, Vol. II. The negative affects.* New York: Springer.

Tomkins, S.S., & McCarter, R. (1964). What and where are the primary affects? Some evidence for a theory. *Perceptual and Motor Skills, 18,* 119–158.

Wagner, B. M., Cohen, P., & Brook, J. S. (1996). Parent/adolescent relationships: Moderators of the effects of stressful life events. *Journal of Adolescent Research, 11,* 347–374.

Wagner, B. M., & Klimes-Dougan, B. (April, 2002). *Emotion regulation in families of adolescents: Concepts, prevention, and treatment.* Workshop presented at the American Association of Suicidology, Washington, DC.

Yap, M. B. H., Allen, N. B., & Ladouceur, C. D. (2008). Maternal socialization of positive affect: The impact of invalidation on adolescent emotion regulation and depressive symptomatology. *Child Development, 79,* 1415–1431.

Yap, M. B. H., Allen, N. B., Leve, C., & Katz, L. F. (2008). Maternal meta-emotion philosophy and socialization of adolescent affect: The moderating role of adolescent temperament. *Journal of Family Psychology, 22,* 688–700.

Zahn-Waxler, C. (2000). The development of empathy, guilt, and internalization of distress. In R. Davidson (Ed.), *Wisconsin Symposium on Emotion: Vol. 1, Anxiety, depression, and emotion* (pp. 222–265). New York: Oxford University Press.

Zahn-Waxler, C., Klimes-Dougan, B., Hastings, P., Duggal, S., Gruber, R., Usher, B., Fox, N., Weissbrod, C., & Zametkin, A. (2001). *The Role of Emotion in the Development of Psychopathology: Protocol #97-M-0116.* Bethesda, MD: National Institute of Mental Health.

Zahn-Waxler, C., Klimes-Dougan, B., & Slattery, M. (2000). Internalizing problems of childhood and adolescence: Prospects, pitfalls, and progress in understanding the development of anxiety and depression. *Development and Psychopathology, 12,* 443–466.

Zeman, J., Klimes-Dougan, B., Cassano, C., & Adrian, M. (2007). Measurement issues in emotion research with children and adolescents. *Clinical Psychology: Science and Practice. 14,* 377–401.

ANN E. BRAND *is an instructor of psychology at Campbell University in Buies Creek, North Carolina. Her research interests include emotion socialization in adolescence, meta-emotion philosophy, and marital relations, and the adjustment of adopted children and adolescents.*

BONNIE KLIMES-DOUGAN *is a visiting professor in the department of psychology at the University of Minnesota. Her research is on developmental trajectories of children and adolescents at risk for depression, with an emphasis on risk and protective processes of the individual (for example, affective, neurocognitive, and physiological processes) and the family (for example, emotion socialization) relevant to emotion regulation. She also researches how problems associated with depression and suicide may be potentially modified by preventive interventions.*

NEW DIRECTIONS FOR CHILD and ADOLESCENT DEVELOPMENT • DOI: 10.1002/cd

Zahn-Waxler, C. (2010). Socialization of emotion: Who influences whom and how? In A. Kennedy Root & S. Denham (Eds.), *The role of gender in the socialization of emotion: Key concepts and critical issues. New Directions for Child and Adolescent Development, 128,* 101–109. San Francisco: Jossey-Bass.

7

Socialization of Emotion: Who Influences Whom and How?

Carolyn Zahn-Waxler

Abstract

Emotion socialization begins within the family setting and extends outward as children transition into expanded social worlds. Children contribute to their socialization from the first years of life, so the dynamics between parents and children are reciprocal in nature. Because socialization influences are best inferred from patterns that unfold over time, longitudinal research can help to untangle these processes. Laboratory observations of emotion exchanges and discussions or experimental manipulations of environmental processes also provide valuable information about causal influences and direction of effects. Parents and children must be studied within the same research designs to understand emotion socialization. © Wiley Periodicals, Inc.

S ocialization refers to the process of learning one's culture and how to live within it. It includes acquisition of moral norms, attitudes, values, roles, language, and symbols that ensure continuity of cultures and societies over the course of time. More recently, the term also has come to include (socialization of) *emotions*. Developmentalists now study aspects of the environment thought to shape the experience, expression, regulation, and understanding of emotions from infancy through adolescence. This begins within the family setting and extends outward as children transition into expanded social worlds. Although most processes in need of socialization are not present at the onset of life, infants enter the world expressing emotions that contribute to their own socialization.

Just over a decade ago Eisenberg, Cumberland, and Spinrad (1998) published a seminal research review and proposed a theoretical model to characterize this newly emerging field. Direct socialization of emotions is thought to consist of parents' expressions of emotions, reactions to children's emotions, and discussions of emotions with their children. Indirect socialization consists of the global family climate of emotions and parents' own expressiveness of emotion during family interactions. The work in this *New Directions for Child and Adolescent Development* issue follows in this tradition. One question is whether this conceptualization fully covers the range of ways emotions are socialized.

The chapters in this issue highlight some important approaches and discoveries that followed the review by Eisenberg, Cumberland, and Spinrad. The cross-cutting themes focus on gender (of both the parent and the child) and the implications of emotion socialization for children's social-emotional competence and development of psychopathology. This commentary considers these themes in the context of other issues to be addressed if research on socialization of emotion is to remain a viable and vigorous scientific enterprise. These issues pertain to (1) conceptualization and measurement of emotion socialization, and (2) the child's role in the socialization process.

Socialization of Emotion and Gender

Despite significant advances, women in all cultures still bear the children and play the greater role as caregivers while men are more involved in positions of authority, power, and defense of country. So it is easy to see why parents might encourage boys and girls to engage in gender-typed patterns of play and household work, as well as to socialize the expression of emotions consistent with these roles (and to suppress inconsistent emotions). For girls, "tender emotions" (empathy, guilt) and positive affect would be especially important. They undergird the patterns of nurturance, affiliation, and responsibility for others required for optimal caregiving and other interpersonal relationships (friendships, social networks). For boys, anger and related outer-directed negative emotions (as well as control of other emotions) help to support activities associated with autonomy, authority, dominance, and combat.

Boys and girls do show gender-linked roles and emotions quite early in development (Zahn-Waxler, Shirtcliff, & Marceau, 2008). Although several studies are consistent with the view that parents help to socialize these differences, there are also biological underpinnings. However, biological differences have largely been ignored in this socialization literature. There are many examples of children's predispositions to self-select activities more common to their own sex. There are fundamental reasons why girls tend to play with dolls and boys with trucks and why these patterns are so impervious to parental intervention. However, boys and girls are similar in many ways and this also is evident in much of the empirical data in this issue. We need to move beyond discussions of gender differences (which can begin to reflect stereotypes) to understand factors that influence the wide range and substantial overlap of experience, expression, and regulation of emotions in females and males.

Socialization of Emotion, Social-Emotional Competence, and Psychopathology

Children's emotional competence is seen as vital to children's adaptive functioning, both within the family unit and importantly when peer relationships begin to assume greater salience in their lives. To negotiate social challenges involved in interacting with difficult peers and building friendships and other relationships, it helps to be emotionally positive, well-regulated, and composed. Positive parental emotion socialization is thought to contribute to these competencies in children, whereas negative emotion socialization is associated with problems in social adjustment.

We know that socialization of emotion has an influence on children as a *group*. In general, children become more regulated and express emotions in ways that are expected. But we still know relatively little about the socialization processes through which parents influence their children at the level of *individual differences* (which is what is typically claimed), or the role that development plays in exerting change. Very few studies are designed in ways that can show a causal role for parents. Well-adjusted children may result from positive parenting or they may elicit more positive emotions in their caregivers. Both are likely and both merit inquiry within the same research design.

Parents are also said to play a socializing role in the development of children's emotional and behavioral problems. Although most of the authors here have not studied these processes directly, they have pointed to the need to extend research to at-risk samples. This is important as most research on emotion socialization focuses on two-parent, middle- and upper-middle class, low-risk samples with little ethnic diversity and mainly from Western cultures. With psychopathology, as with social competence we need to establish criteria for demonstrating that parental socialization actually influences child and youth outcomes. This is still a murky process. Further complications arise as we try to explain how different socialization approaches might influence different kinds of emotions that would, in turn, influence the different kinds of problems (for example internalizing versus externalizing) children and adolescents develop.

Some have argued that socialization emphases on different emotions in boys and girls may eventually create a diathesis toward more problematic internalizing emotions in girls (sadness, fear/anxiety) and externalizing emotions in boys (anger/hostility). Sex differences in problems and disorders associated with these emotions are robust (Zahn-Waxler and others, 2008), but they are present in a minority of children and adolescents. There is little evidence that parents' socialization practices actively contribute to these differences because studies are typically restricted to one time point. Although parents often show negative emotion socialization with offspring with internalizing and externalizing problems, difficult children are well known to evoke more negative parenting practices. Longitudinal research designs are needed to address these issues.

There is growing consensus that most serious psychopathology is not caused by parents (unless environmental conditions are horrific as in child maltreatment). Problems can result, however, when environmental stressors (including negative emotion socialization practices) have an adverse impact on preexisting vulnerabilities that include heightened negative emotionality. These interactions merit inquiry.

Conceptualization and Measurement of Emotion Socialization

The prevailing view that there are two basic types of socialization of emotion, direct and indirect, requires further examination, as does the fact that most of the research still focuses only on direct processes. Indirect processes such as marital conflict and parental mental illness can have a profound impact on children's emotions and adaptation and need to receive more research time. Moreover, direct and indirect processes are not fully separable. Conflicted or mentally ill parents also express specific emotions; when are these processes direct and when are they indirect? There are still other aspects of emotion socialization that do not fall under the rubric of the more circumscribed definition. These include global warmth and hostility and quality of attachment to the child. They also include childrearing strategies and discipline techniques intended to alter behavior patterns rather than emotions per se. However, these approaches still will have an emotional impact (slapping a child's face, withdrawing love).

NEW DIRECTIONS FOR CHILD and ADOLESCENT DEVELOPMENT • DOI: 10.1002/cd

We need to find more powerful ways to tap into emotion socialization. Typically, our laboratory paradigms provide only brief glimpses into underlying family dynamics. The range of emotional reactions studied in both parents and children is more constrained, sanitized, and simplified than what occurs in their everyday lives. With the emphasis on discrete emotions we know relatively little about environmental processes and child characteristics that contribute to co-occurrences of emotions. Yet co-occurrences and blends of emotions are much more common than discrete emotions in the lives of children and their caregivers.

In natural settings, separation from the caregiver can simultaneously elicit anger, fear, and sadness. Situations of frustration and disappointment can elicit both anger and sadness in the same child. When the caregiver responds to the child in these kinds of situations, are discrete emotions being socialized or is it negative emotionality in general? Watson and Clark (1992) have argued that negative affect has both separable and inseparable aspects. How do we incorporate both of these realities into research on negative emotions and their socialization? Moreover, though emotions per se are not dysfunctional, negative emotions often have dysfunctional qualities of high intensity, long duration, and situational inappropriateness. When we ask parents separate questions about how they respond to fear, sadness, and anger in their children, we may fail to capture important variations, complexities, and co-occurrences of emotions.

The Child's Role in the Socialization Process

Most socialization research assumes that what parents do with and to their children affects many different aspects of their lives. At one level this is a given. Children learn to adopt certain standards, skills, norms, and behaviors and to regulate emotions (with varying success) in ways consistent with the mores and values of their culture. And parents are integral to these processes. Few still take the extreme position (Harris, 1995) that parents do not really matter and that children are socialized primarily by peers. Animal studies show that maternal socialization profoundly affects emotionality and well-being of offspring (see review by Anisman, Merali, & Stead, 2008).

Parents with more than one child are very aware of how their children differ in terms of temperament and personality from the first years of life. These differences influence how parents respond, which in turn may have different effects on the children. We have known for over four decades, based on the groundbreaking work of Richard Bell on child effects (1968) that socialization influences are bidirectional and that the child plays a prominent role in these socialization experiences. Again, direct socialization of emotion in the form of parents' *reactions to* children's emotions could simply reflect the fact that children's emotions influence those of their parents. Children vary enormously in the expression and regulation of emotions (positive and negative) and this can be as likely to influence the parent as the parent's reactions are to influence the child.

So what can we do? Because socialization influences are best inferred from patterns that unfold over time, longitudinal research can help to untangle these processes. Laboratory observations of emotion exchanges and discussions or experimental manipulations of environmental processes also provide information about causal influences and direction of effect. But, because most research that examines associations between parents and children is based on correlational designs at one time point, evidence for socialization is still suggestive. This has long been acknowledged, but typically in a rather token manner. We have begun to reach our limits, however, in terms of what we can conclude with existing research models, paradigms, and procedures.

As a thought experiment we should consider what would be lost if we stopped using the concept *emotion socialization* to describe processes that may or may not represent socialization. At least this would force us to consider more carefully the claims we make based on existing research designs. There is, however, hope on the horizon. Longitudinal studies have begun to show parenting effects relevant to emotion socialization over and above child effects when dyads are followed over time (Brand, Klimes-Dougan, Zahn-Waxler, & Usher, 2009; Chaplin, Cole, & Zahn-Waxler, 2005; Denham et al., 2000).

Lessons and Examples from the Research on Prosocial and Moral Development

The basic or discrete emotions of pleasure/joy, sadness, anger, and fear emerge in the first year of life. Social or moral emotions such as empathy, guilt, and shame emerge in the second and third years. During this period, parents begin to hold children accountable for their actions and to socialize appropriate interpersonal behavior. In contrast to the primary emotions, they have not been studied within an emotion socialization framework—even though they are sensitive to social influences. This is suggested by longitudinal research on prosocial and moral development.

Maternal displays of negative emotion and negative control have been shown to predict decrements in children's empathy from 14 to 20 months of age (Robinson, Zahn-Waxler, & Emde, 1994). Temperament also played a role with children's early sociability, predicting increases in empathy over the same period. With regard to parental discipline, Zahn-Waxler, Radke-Yarrow, and King (1979) found that mother's affectively toned (but not neutral) explanations predicted children's caring expressions toward others in distress 4.5 months later during the second year of life. In another study (Kochanska,1991), specific socialization practices used with toddlers predicted expressions of guilt and conscience six years later; moreover, different socialization approaches were required depending on the child's temperament. In other research, antisocial behavior (failure to adhere to moral norms) decreased by middle childhood in angry, defiant preschool children whose mothers were nurturant and low on hostility (Hastings et al., 2000; Denham et al., 2000).

These studies took into account important child characteristics, making it plausible to infer effects of socialization over and above child factors. Again, the parental practices do not fit precisely within the typical frameworks for studying emotion socialization. Yet they clearly have an affective component: hence, they also tap elements of emotion socialization that can contribute to individual differences in children's social–moral emotions (e.g., empathy, guilt/conscience) or in reductions in antisocial behaviors and related emotions.

Conclusions and Future Directions

The impact of our research will be limited if we continue (1) to study only one side of the socialization process (parent to child) and not the other (child to parent), and (2) to ignore the presence of reciprocal influences within these dyads. We can begin to change this by also measuring children's emotions or temperament and conducting short-term and long-term longitudinal studies. The only way we can know if socialization has an effect is to measure *both* parent and child reactions at more than one time point, to examine change over time in *both* members of the dyad, and to attempt to ascertain who is influencing whom and how (Ge et al., 1995).

We also need to find other ways to study the interactions of nature and nurture. It would be valuable to engage in interdisciplinary collaborations with investigators who focus on biological processes. This kind of work is already being done by researchers interested in other aspects of socialization or life experiences and how they interact with different genotypes identified by molecular geneticists (Caspi et al., 2002; Knafo, 2009).

No one paradigm, design, or methodology can provide a basis for unequivocal interpretations and generalizations. So we have to take a multipronged approach that can provide converging patterns of evidence based on an array of approaches. This includes the already noted use of short- and long-term longitudinal studies, as well as in-depth observations of interactions between parents and offspring, in both naturalistic and seminaturalistic settings (for example, structured to elicit particular emotions). Thoughtfully constructed experimental paradigms are essential as well.

Collectively the authors of the chapters in this issue have provided a valuable update on the conceptual and empirical literature on direct and indirect parental socialization of emotion. They have used creative approaches to study emotion socialization. Several findings are tantalizing, as are the interpretations offered. However, the authors recognize the exploratory nature of research reported. Consistent with the goals of *New Directions for Child and Adolescent Development,* the primary purpose of the issue is to provide in-depth discussions on a focused topic, presenting data mainly for illustrative purposes. Many findings reported here were not statistically significant or were of borderline significance. Hypotheses often were not confirmed and sometimes ran counter to expectations in ways not always readily understood. Because of the necessary brevity of descriptions of procedures and analyses it is not possible to provide the same level of scrutiny as is done for typical empirical articles. Thus, we need to treat results as preliminary and in need of replication before providing commentary about specific findings. The strength of this fine collection of papers does not rest on the robustness of the empirical data. Rather it resides in future research questions that have emerged in the course of these research initiatives. This cadre of talented investigators and their students now have the opportunity to pursue this next level of questions and issues regarding socialization of emotions.

References

Anisman, H., Merali, Z., & Stead, J. D. H. (2008). Experiential and genetic contributions to depressive and anxiety-like disorders: Clinical and experimental studies. *Neuroscience and Biobehavioral Reviews, 32,* 1185–1206.

Bell, R. Q. (1968). A reinterpretation of the direction of effects in studies of socialization. *Psychological Review, 75,* 81–95.

Brand, A., Klimes-Dougan, B, Zahn-Waxler, C., &Usher, B. (2009). Parent-adolescent discussion of sad and worrisome events: Sex and developmental differences in parental socialization of emotion. SRCD Symposium presentation, Denver, Colorado (April 1–4, 2009).

Caspi, A., McClay, J., Moffitt, T. E., Mill, J., Martin, J., Craig, I. W., Taylor, A., & Poulon, R. (2002). The role of genotype in the cycle of violence in maltreated children. *Science, 297,* 5582, 851–854.

Chaplin, T., Cole, P. M., & Zahn-Waxler, C. (2005). Parental socialization of emotion Expression: Gender differences and relations to child adjustment. *Emotion,* 80–88.

Denham, S. A., Workman, E., Cole, P. M., Weissbrod, C., Kendziora, K. T., and Zahn-Waxler, C. (2000). Prediction of behavior problems from early to middle childhood: The role of parental socialization and emotion expression. *Development and Psychopathology, 12,* 23–45.

Eisenberg, N., Cumberland, A., & Spinrad, T.L. (1998). Parental socialization of emotion. *Psychological Inquiry, 9,* 241–273.

Ge, X., Conger, R. D., Lorenz, F. O., Shanahan, M., & Elder, G. E. (1995). Mutual influences in parent and adolescent psychological distress. *Developmental Psychology, 31,* 406–419.

Harris, J. R. (1995). Where is the child's environment: A group socialization theory of development. *Psychological Review, 102,* 458–489.

Hastings, P. D., Zahn-Waxler, C., Robinson, J. L., Usher, B., & Bridges, D. (2000). The development of concern for others in children with behavior problems. *Developmental Psychology, 36(5)*, 531–546.

Knafo, A. (2009). Prosocial development: The intertwined roles of children's genetics and their parental environment. Invited Address. SRCD, Denver, CO. April 1–4.

Kochanska, G. (1991). Socialization and temperament in the development of guilt and conscience. *Child Development, 62*, 1379–1392.

Robinson, J. L., Zahn-Waxler, C., & Emde, R. N. (1994). Patterns of development in early empathic behavior: Environmental and child constitutional differences. *Social Development, 3*, 125–145.

Watson, D., & Clark, L. A. (1992). Affects separable and inseparable: On the hierarchical arrangement of the negative affects. *Journal of Personality and Social Psychology, 62*, 489–505.

Zahn-Waxler, C., Radke-Yarrow, M., & King, R. A. (1979). Childrearing and children's prosocial initiations toward victims of distress. *Child Development, 50*, 319–330.

Zahn-Waxler, C., Shirtcliff, E. A., & Marceau, K. (2008). Disorders of childhood and adolescence: Gender and psychopathology. *Annual Review of Clinical Psychology, 4*, 11.2–11.29.

CAROLYN ZAHN-WAXLER is a senior scientist of psychology and psychiatry at the University of Wisconsin. Her research interests center on the development of empathy and prosociality, gender and psychopathology, developmental precursors of depression, and socialization and social-emotional development.

INDEX

development. This volume of *New Directions for Child and Adolescent Development* highlights new research in this area that focuses on evidentials: word affixes and sentence particles that indicate the speaker's source of knowledge—for example, perception, inference, or hearsay. Evidentials are a feature of about a quarter of the languages in the world and have a variety of interesting characteristics. For example, in contrast to lexical alternatives familiar from English, such as "I saw," they are extremely frequent. The volume brings together scholars pioneering research on evidentiality in Bulgarian, Japanese, Tibetan, and Turkish. Their contributions to this volume provide a glimpse at the diversity of evidential systems around the globe while examining a number of provocative questions: How do evidentials mediate children's acquisition of knowledge from others' testimony? What is the relation between grammaticalized and lexical expressions of source of knowledge? Does the acquisition of an evidential system boost source monitoring and inferential skills? The volume is a compelling illustration of the relevance of evidentiality to broadening our understanding of development in many domains, including theory of mind, memory, and knowledge acquisition.
ISBN 978-04705-69658

CAD124 **Coping and the Development of Regulation**
Ellen A. Skinner, Melanie J. Zimmer-Gembeck, Editors
A developmental conceptualization that emphasizes coping as regulation under stress opens the way to explore synergies between coping and regulatory processes, including self-regulation; behavioral, emotion, attention, and action regulation; ego control; self-control; compliance; and volition. This volume, with chapters written by experts on the development of regulation and coping during childhood and adolescence, is the first to explore these synergies. The volume is geared toward researchers working in the broad areas of regulation, coping, stress, adversity, and resilience. For regulation researchers, it offers opportunities to focus on age-graded changes in how these processes function under stress and to consider multiple targets of regulation simultaneously—emotion, attention, behavior—that typically are examined in isolation. For researchers interested in coping, this volume offers invigorating theoretical and operational ideas. For researchers studying stress, adversity, and resilience, the volume highlights coping as one pathway through which exposure to adversity shapes children's long-term development. The authors also address cross-cutting developmental themes, such as the role of stress, coping, and social relationships in the successive integration of regulatory subsystems, the emergence of autonomous regulation, and the progressive construction of the kinds of regulatory resources and routines that allow flexible constructive coping under successively higher levels of stress and adversity. All chapters emphasize the importance of integrative multilevel perspectives in bringing together work on the neurobiology of stress, temperament, attachment, regulation, personal resources, relationships, stress exposure, and social contexts in studying processes of coping, adversity, and resilience.
ISBN 978-04705-31372

CAD 123 **Social Interaction and the Development of Executive Function**
Charlie Lewis, Jeremy I. M. Carpendale, Editors
Executive function consists of higher cognitive skills that are involved in the control of thought, action, and emotion. It has been linked to neural systems involving the prefrontal cortex, but a full definition of the term has remained elusive partly because it includes such a complex set of cognitive processes. Relatively little is known about the processes that promote development of exec-

utive function, and how it is linked to children's social behavior. The key factor examined by the chapters in this issue is the role of social interaction, and the chapters take an increasingly broad perspective. Two end pieces introduce the topic as a whole (Chapter 1) and present an integrative commentary on the articles (Chapter 6) in an attempt to stress the social origins of executive function, in contrast to many contemporary cognitive approaches. The empirical contributions in between examine the roles of parental scaffolding of young preschoolers (Chapter 2), the links between maternal education and conversational support (Chapter 3), how such family background factors and social skills extend into adolescence (Chapter 4), and wider cultural influences (Chapter 5) on development of executive skills. This volume is aimed at a broad range of developmental researchers and practitioners interested in the influences of family background and interactions as well as educational and cultural processes on development of the child's self-control and social understanding. Such relationships have wide implications for many aspects of the lives of children and adolescents.
ISBN 978-04704-89017

CAD 122 **Core Competencies to Prevent Problem Behaviors and Promote Positive Youth Development**
Nancy G. Guerra, Catherine P. Bradshaw, Editors
Adolescence generally is considered a time of experimentation and increased involvement in risk or problem behaviors, including early school leaving, violence, substance use, and high-risk sexual behavior. In this volume, the authors show how individual competencies linked to well-being can reduce youth involvement in these risk behaviors. Five core competencies are emphasized: a positive sense of self, self-control, decision-making skills, a moral system of belief, and prosocial connectedness. A central premise of this volume is that high levels of the core competencies provide a marker for positive youth development, whereas low levels increase the likelihood of adolescent risk behavior. The authors summarize the empirical literature linking these competencies to each risk behavior, providing examples from developmental and prevention research. They highlight programs and policies in the United States and internationally that have changed one or more dimensions of the core competencies through efforts designed to build individual skills, strengthen relationships, and enhance opportunities and supports across multiple developmental contexts.
ISBN 978-04704-42166

CAD 121 **Beyond the Family: Contexts of Immigrant Children's Development**
Hirokazu Yoshikawa, Niobe Way, Editors
Immigration in the United States has become a central focus of policy and public concern in the first decade of the 21st century. This volume aims to broaden developmental research on children and youth in immigrant families. Much of the research on immigrant children and youth concentrates on family characteristics such as parenting, demographic, or human capital features. In this volume, we consider the developmental consequences for immigrant youth of broader contexts such as social networks, peer discrimination in school and out-of-school settings, legal contexts, and access to institutional resources. Chapters answer questions such as: How do experiences of discrimination affect the lives of immigrant youth? How do social networks of immigrant families influence children's learning? How do immigrant parents' citizenship status influence family life and their children's development? In examining factors as disparate as discrimination based on physical appearance, informal adult helpers, and access to drivers' licenses, these chapters serve to enrich our notions of how culture and context shape

human development, as well as inform practice and public policy affecting immigrant families.

ISBN 978-04704-17300

CAD 120 **The Intersections of Personal and Social Identities**
Margarita Azmitia, Moin Syed, Kimberley Radmacher, Editors
This volume brings together an interdisciplinary set of social scientists who are pioneering ways to research and theorize the connections between personal and social identity development in children, adolescents, and emerging adults. The authors of the seven chapters address the volume's three goals: (1) illustrating how theory and research in identity develop-ment are enriched by an interdisciplinary approach, (2) providing a rich developmental picture of personal and social identity development, and (3) examining the connections among multiple identities. Several chapters provide practical suggestions for individuals, agencies, and schools and universities that work with children, adolescents, and emerging adults in diverse communities across the United States.
ISBN 978-04703-72838

CAD 119 **Social Class and Transitions to Adulthood**
Jeylan T. Mortimer, Editor
This volume of *New Directions for Child and Adolescent Development* is inspired by a stirring address that Frank Furstenberg delivered at the 2006 Meeting of the Society for Research on Adolescence, "Diverging Development: The Not So Invisible Hand of Social Class in the United States." He called on social scientists interested in the study of development to expand their purview beyond investigations of the developmental impacts of poverty and consider the full gamut of social class variation in our increasingly unequal society. The gradations of class alter the social supports, resources, and opportunities, as well as the constraints, facing parents as they attempt to guide their children toward the acquisition of adult roles. This volume examines the impacts of social class origin on the highly formative period of transition to adulthood. Drawing on findings from the Youth Development Study and other sources, the authors examine social class differences in adult child–parent relationships, intimacy and family formation, attainment of higher education, the school-to-work transition, the emergence of work-family conflict, and harassment in the workplace. The authors indicate new directions for research that will contribute to understanding the problems facing young people today. These chapters will persuade those making social policy to develop social interventions that will level the playing field and increase the opportunities for disadvantaged youth to become healthy and productive adults.
ISBN 978-04702-93621

CAD 118 **Social Network Analysis and Children's Peer Relationships**
Philip C. Rodkin, Laura D. Hanish, Editors
Social network analysis makes it possible to determine how large and dense children's peer networks are, how central children are within their networks, the various structural configurations that characterize social groups, and which peers make up individual children's networks. By centering the child within his or her social system, it is possible to understand the socialization processes that draw children toward or away from particular peers, as well as those who contribute to peer influence. This volume of *New Directions for Child and Adolescent Development* demonstrates how social network analysis provides insights into the ways in which peer groups contribute to children's and adolescents' development—from gender and intergroup relations, to aggression and bullying, to academic achievement. Together the chapters in this

volume depict the complex, nested, and dynamic structure of peer groups and explain how social structure defines developmental processes.
ISBN 978-04702-59665

CAD 117 **Attachment in Adolescence: Reflections and New Angles**
Miri Scharf, Ofra Mayseless, Editors
In recent years, the number of empirical studies examining attachment in adolescence has grown considerably, with most focusing on individual differences in attachment security. This volume goes a step further in extending our knowledge and understanding. The physical, cognitive, emotional, and social changes that characterize adolescence invite a closer conceptual look at attachment processes and organization during this period. The chapter authors, leading researchers in attachment in adolescence, address key topics in attachment processes in adolescence. These include issues such as the normative distancing from parents and the growing importance of peers, the formation of varied attachment hierarchies, the changing nature of attachment dynamics from issues of survival to issues of affect regulation, siblings' similarity in attachment representations, individual differences in social information processes in adolescence, and stability and change in attachment representations in a risk sample. Together the chapters provide a compelling discussion of intriguing issues and broaden our understanding of attachment in adolescence and the basic tenets of attachment theory at large.
ISBN 978-04702-25608

CAD 116 **Linking Parents and Family to Adolescent Peer Relations: Ethnic and Cultural Considerations**
B. Bradford Brown, Nina S. Mounts, Editors
Ethnic and cultural background shapes young people's development and behavior in a variety of ways, including their interactions with family and peers. The intersection of family and peer worlds during childhood has been studied extensively, but only recently has this work been extended to adolescence. This volume of *New Directions for Child and Adolescent Development* highlights new research linking family to adolescent peer relations from a multiethnic perspective. Using qualitative and quantitative research methods, the contributors consider similarities and differences within and between ethnic groups in regard to several issues: parents' goals and strategies for guiding young people to adaptive peer relationships, how peer relationships shape and are shaped by kin relationships, and the specific strategies that adolescents and parents use to manage information about peers or negotiate rules about peer interactions and relationships. Findings emphasize the central role played by sociocultural context in shaping the complex, bidirectional processes that link family members to adolescents' peer social experiences.
ISBN 978-04701-78010

CAD 115 **Conventionality in Cognitive Development: How Children Acquire Shared Representations in Language, Thought, and Action**
Chuck W. Kalish, Mark A. Sabbagh, Editors
An important part of cognitive development is coming to think in culturally normative ways. Children learn the right names for objects, proper functions for tools, appropriate ways to categorize, and the rules for games. In each of these cases, what makes a given practice normative is not naturally given. There is not necessarily any objectively better or worse way to do any of these things. Instead, what makes them correct is that people agree on how they should be done, and each of these practices therefore has an important conventional basis. The chapters in this volume highlight the fact that successful participation in practices of language, cognition, and play depends on children's ability to

acquire representations that other members of their social worlds share. Each of these domains poses problems of identifying normative standards and achieving coordination across agents. This volume brings together scholars from diverse areas in cognitive development to consider the psychological mechanisms supporting the use and acquisition of conventional knowledge.
ISBN 978-07879-96970

CAD 114 **Respect and Disrespect: Cultural and Developmental Origins**
David W. Schwalb, Barbara J. Schwalb, Editors
Respect enables children and teenagers to value other people, institutions, traditions, and themselves. Disrespect is the agent that dissolves positive relationships and fosters hostile and cynical relationships. Unfortunately, parents, educators, children, and adolescents in many societies note with alarm a growing problem of disrespect and a decline in respect for self and others. Is this disturbing trend a worldwide problem? To answer this question, we must begin to study the developmental and cultural origins of respect and disrespect. Five research teams report that respect and disrespect are influenced by experiences in the family, school, community, and, most importantly, the broader cultural setting. The chapters introduce a new topic area for mainstream developmental sciences that is relevant to the interests of scholars, educators, practitioners, and policymakers.
ISBN 978-07879-95584

CAD 113 **The Modernization of Youth Transitions in Europe**
Manuela du Bois-Reymond, Lynne Chisholm, Editors
This compelling volume focuses on what it is like to be young in the rapidly changing, enormously diverse world region that is early 21st century Europe. Designed for a North American readership interested in youth and young adulthood, *The Modernization of Youth Transitions in Europe* provides a rich fund of theoretical insight and empirical evidence about the implications of contemporary modernization processes for young people living, learning, and working across Europe. Chapters have been specially written for this volume by well-known youth sociologists; they cover a wide range of themes against a shared background of the reshaping of the life course and its constituent phases toward greater openness and contigency. New modes of learning accompany complex routes into employment and career under rapidly changing labor market conditions and occupational profiles, while at the same time new family and lifestyle forms are developing alongside greater intergenerational responsibilities in the face of the retreat of the modern welfare state. The complex patterns of change for today's young Europeans are set into a broader framework that analyzes the emergence and character of European youth research and youth policy in recent years.
ISBN 978-07879-88890

CAD 112 **Rethinking Positive Adolescent Female Sexual Development**
Lisa M. Diamond, Editor
This volume provides thoughtful and diverse perspectives on female adolescent sexuality. These perspectives integrate biological, cultural, and interpersonal influences on adolescent girls' sexuality, and highlight the importance of using multiple methods to investigate sexual ideation and experience. Traditional portrayals cast adolescent females as sexual gatekeepers whose primary task is to fend off boys' sexual overtures and set aside their own sexual desires in order to reduce their risks for pregnancy and sexually transmitted diseases. Yet an increasing number of thoughtful and constructive critiques have challenged this perspective, arguing for more sensitive, in-depth, multimethod investigations into the positive meanings of sexuality for adolescent

girls that will allow us to conceptualize (and, ideally, advocate for) healthy sexual-developmental trajectories. Collectively, authors of this volume take up this movement and chart exciting new directions for the next generation of developmental research on adolescent female sexuality.
ISBN 978-07879-87350

CAD 111 **Family Mealtime as a Context for Development and Socialization**
Reed W. Larson, Angela R. Wiley, Kathryn R. Branscomb, Editors
This issue examines the impact of family mealtime on the psychological development of young people. In the popular media, family mealtime is often presented as a vital institution for the socialization and development of young people, but also as one that is "going the way of the dinosaur." Although elements such as fast food and TV have become a part of many family mealtimes, evidence is beginning to suggest that mealtimes can also provide rich opportunities for children's and adolescents' development. While what happens at mealtimes varies greatly among families, an outline of the forms and functions of mealtimes is beginning to emerge from this research. In this issue, leading mealtime researchers from the fields of history, cultural anthropology, psycholinguistics, psychology, and nutrition critically review findings from each of their disciplines, giving primary focus on family mealtimes in the United States. The authors in this issue examine the history of family mealtimes, describe contemporary mealtime practices, elucidate the differing transactional processes that occur, and evaluate evidence on the outcomes associated with family mealtimes from children and adolescents.
ISBN 978-07879-85776

CAD 110 **Leaks in the Pipeline to Math, Science, and Technology Careers**
Janis E. Jacobs, Sandra D. Simpkins, Editors
Around the world, the need for highly trained scientists and technicians remains high, especially for positions that require employees to have a college degree and skills in math, science, and technology. The pipeline into these jobs begins in high school, but many "leaks" occur before young people reach the highly educated workforce needed to sustain leadership in science and technology. Students drop out of the educational pipeline in science and technology at alarming rates at each educational transition beginning in high school, but women and ethnic minority youth drop out at a faster rate. Women and minorities are consistently underrepresented in science and engineering courses and majors. They account for a small portion of the work force in high-paying and more innovative jobs that require advanced degrees. This schism between the skills necessary in our ever-changing economy and the skill set that most young adults acquire is troubling. It leads us to ask the question that forms the basis for this issue: Why are adolescents and young adults, particularly women and minorities, opting out of the math, science, and technology pipeline? The volume addresses gender and ethnic differences in the math, science, and technology pipeline from multiple approaches, including theoretical perspectives, a review of the work in this field, presentation of findings from four longitudinal studies, and a discussion of research implications given the current educational and economic climate.
ISBN 978-07879-83932

NEW DIRECTIONS FOR CHILD & ADOLESCENT DEVELOPMENT

ORDER FORM SUBSCRIPTION AND SINGLE ISSUES

DISCOUNTED BACK ISSUES:

Use this form to receive 20% off all back issues of *New Directions for Child & Adolescent Development*.
All single issues priced at **$23.20** (normally $29.00)

TITLE	ISSUE NO.	ISBN

*Call 888-378-2537 or see mailing instructions below. When calling, mention the promotional code JB9ND
to receive your discount. For a complete list of issues, please visit www.josseybass.com/go/ndcad*

SUBSCRIPTIONS: (1 YEAR, 4 ISSUES)

☐ New Order ☐ Renewal

U.S.	☐ Individual: $85	☐ Institutional: $280
CANADA/MEXICO	☐ Individual: $85	☐ Institutional: $320
ALL OTHERS	☐ Individual: $109	☐ Institutional: $354

*Call 888-378-2537 or see mailing and pricing instructions below.
Online subscriptions are available at www.interscience.wiley.com*

ORDER TOTALS:

Issue / Subscription Amount: $ _____

Shipping Amount: $ _____
(for single issues only – subscription prices include shipping)

Total Amount: $ _____

SHIPPING CHARGES:		
SURFACE	DOMESTIC	CANADIAN
First Item	$5.00	$6.00
Each Add'l Item	$3.00	$1.50

*(No sales tax for U.S. subscriptions. Canadian residents, add GST for subscription orders. Individual rate subscriptions must
be paid by personal check or credit card. Individual rate subscriptions may not be resold as library copies.)*

BILLING & SHIPPING INFORMATION:

☐ **PAYMENT ENCLOSED:** *(U.S. check or money order only. All payments must be in U.S. dollars.)*

☐ **CREDIT CARD:** ☐ VISA ☐ MC ☐ AMEX

Card number _____ Exp. Date_____

Card Holder Name_____ Card Issue #_____

Signature _____ Day Phone_____

☐ **BILL ME:** *(U.S. institutional orders only. Purchase order required.)*

Purchase order #_____
      Federal Tax ID 13559302 • GST 89102-8052

Name_____

Address_____

Phone_____ E-mail_____

Copy or detach page and send to: **John Wiley & Sons, PTSC, 5th Floor
989 Market Street, San Francisco, CA 94103-174**

Order Form can also be faxed to: **888-481-2665**

PROMO JB9N